"*Whispers in the Silence* is a book that invites us to travel the road of spirit. It teaches us that what we all seek, that being inner peace and contentment, can only truly happen with the cultivation of our own soul. John challenges us to turn our search inward and begin to listen to the answers our souls have for us."

Jack Bloomfield
One Planet United

Whispers in the Silence

Whispers in the Silence

Living by the Light of Your Soul

John Dennison

Whispers in the Silence — Living by the Light of Your Soul
© 2005 by John Dennison

Interior Design by Day to Day Enterprises
Cover Design by Samantha C. Wall
Index by Willard & Associates

All rights reserved. No part of this publication may be reproduced, stored in a retrieval system or transmitted in any form by any means electronic, mechanical, photocopying, recording or otherwise, except brief extracts for the purpose of review, without the permission of the publisher and copyright owner.

ISBN: 1-932986-71-5

10 9 8 7 6 5 4 3 2

Library of Congress Cataloging-in-Publication Data

Dennison, John, 1952-
  Whispers in the silence : living by the light of your soul / by John Dennison.
    p. cm.
Includes bibliographical references and index.
  ISBN 1-932986-71-5 (alk. paper)
  1. Spiritual life. I. Title.
BL24.D38865 2005
204'.4—dc22
                                    2004015167

Printed in the United States of America

ATTENTION RELIGIOUS AND SPIRITUAL ORGANIZATIONS, CORPORATIONS, UNIVERSITIES, AND PROFESSIONAL GROUPS: Quantity discounts are available on bulk purchase of this book for education, gift purposes, or as premiums for events or increasing magazine subscription or renewals. For order contact us at bulksales@WhisperZone.org

For more information on how to find peace as you travel the path of your awakening, visit http://www.WhisperZone.org.

Published by Whisper Zone, LLC, Coral Springs, Florida

May The Love That I Am Light The Way for All

*With special thanks to Thor, Shakespeare, and those many other souls
Who shined the light of their love upon my path*

This work is dedicated

To Laura, my bride of so many years,

I give my deepest thanks,

and call down all the blessings of the Light upon you,

for without your love, encouragement, support, and inspiration,

none of this would have been possible.

Table of Contents

The Peace That Waits

Introduction 3
The Way of Love 9
A World Gone Awry 13
A Great Wind is Blowing 19
Sleepwalking 25
The Precipice 29

Awakening

Alone 39
From Dissatisfaction to Despair 41
The Quest 45
Giving Up – And Giving In 51
Seek What the Master Sought 55
Why Me? 59

The Nature of Man

A Story of Creation 65
Journey to the Soul 69
A Puzzle Without Pieces 73

Cultivation

Introduction to Cultivation 77
Free Will 83
Living in the Moment 89
Love 95
The Lieutenants of Love 101
Do No Harm 109
Be Truthful 113
Do Not Steal 117

Losing Desire 119
Construct the Temple..123
Breaking Attachment...131
Overcoming Emotions 135
Moving Beyond the Senses 143
Meditation 149
The Light...153
Listening to Your Soul..155
The Power of Intention 159
Belief..163

Living in the Light

On Relationships..167
Living with Passion 173
The Tortoise and The Hare 177
Life is a Classroom 181
Come From Where You Are 185
The Difficult Path 189
Afterword...195
Take the Next Step - A Message from John....................201
Index..203

Table of Verse

The Bold Rider 7
Cocoon 26
Accord 27
Breath Break 32
Whispers in the Darkness 34
Why So Hard? 39
The Ring 42
All Within Reach 44
Why Do I Believe? 48
Fear 51
Sacrifice 52
Fear and Hope 54
Born to Roam 77
The Mirror 78
Caught Between Worlds 84
Life's Mountain 90
Life's Bucket 92
Thanks 93
What is Love? 96
The Key 97
Hide the Children 102
The Gods 104
Truth? 114
What's Mine? 118
Expectations 137
The Flower Wakes 147
Faith 164
Like Ships In The Night 168
Desire 169
What Else Is There? 174
Passion's Flower 175
Atlas 189
I Walk But Once 192

The Peace That Waits

Introduction

This is a life of discontent. We do not know ourselves, much less the God of which we have been taught since childhood. We crave peace, but do not know what that peace looks like, much less how to find it. We long for happiness, but know only the few minutes of pleasure that fortuitously come our way. We search for meaning and direction in our lives, and to find fulfillment in what we do. And we hope against hope that the death of these bodies will not bring the end of our existence.

We suffer this discontent because our minds are turned outward, deaf to the voice that whispers from the silence within. Our inner world is ignored; we are either unaware of its existence or take it for granted because we do not know that is where we are meant to be. Caught in the swirling outer storms that fill our days, we struggle from moment to moment just to survive, unable to know or serve the very reason for our being here in this world.

So caught up are we in this outer world that we fill our lives in pursuit of money and things, along with a few relationships created by our circumstances of birth or choice. We know they will not bring us the peace we crave, yet we cast our fate to the winds of materialism in hope its mantra will fill our inner void. So we chase our needs and desires, all the while gathering experiences that we tuck safely away in our banks of memories until we dutifully pull them out for review. Knowing no better, we raise our children to blindly follow our course and so succeeding generations can do more of the same. These are the lives we build for ourselves. Is there any wonder we are not content?

It would be bad enough if these were personal problems limited to our own dissatisfaction with life. Unfortunately, they shape the world in which we live, rippling outward to color all within our reach. From our families to the social groups to which we belong, our discord sows its seeds in every relationship we touch. Anger and conflict mark the days of our lives, yet we know neither from where they come nor how to deal with them. Worse, our selfish and hollow ways are reflected in the communities and nations in which we live, and spread outward to fuel the conflicts between nations in our world.

There is another way!

Peace will be yours if you seek it. When you find it, a whole new world will open before you, a world of meaning and purpose for both you and all of mankind. This is the world of the spirit, revealed through the soul.

Much of what you hear will seem strange. Then again, isn't every new thing strange until it becomes familiar? But some of what you hear will not be strange at all, and will trigger feelings you have hidden inside and suppressed for so long.

This book is a story of hope; it maps the journey on which that hope will take you. It is a journey to know yourself, and in so knowing to undertake the great transformation that paves the way for the spirit to act in your life.

You will learn why so many have taught the ways of love, and how its lack shapes our technological world. You will be told of a great wind that blows across the land, and given a peek beyond the dream that now covers your eyes. And you will hear why now is the time for you to awaken from this dream, and the steps you must take to do so. But most of all, you will be taught the "secrets" of the ages so that you can travel the path of learning followed by so many masters before you.

As you learn and apply these secrets, no longer will you see life the same. Your perception of this world will change as you do. And you will change the attitude you bring to life as you experience the wonder of each moment from the perspective of your soul. You will no longer just go through the motions, content to tread day after day in drudgery chasing who-knows-what. Each day will become a new and exciting adventure, sometimes frustrating but always growing in service of your mission in life.

New concepts will be laid before you, some of which will challenge all that you hold dear. Others will pull together the disparate wisdom of the ages from which you have taken a piece here and a piece there to build the foundation of your life. As you learn, perhaps you will even examine your old ways, and with that examination will come a choice. Will you remain as you are, locked in discontent? Or will you begin to consciously walk the path of light and undertake your own transformation? You will suddenly see, perhaps for the first time, that the responsibility for your life is yours, shaped by the decisions you make, and the direction in which you apply your zest for living.

I will not attempt to solve the problems of your life, for that would do you a great disservice by enabling your dependency on the outer world. However, I will help you discover the answers so you can fix them for yourself. Your voyage is one of self-discovery, through which all that you need will be revealed.

You will examine the underpinnings of your life, and decide if they serve your journey. If not, you will learn how to choose what should replace them. Emotions, health, personality characteristics, work, recreation, and relationships will all be fair game as you finally see those aspects of you that they reflect. For though you will work in this outer world, you can only know it by first knowing you. And when you see something in it that needs changed, you will know you can do so only by first changing yourself.

This journey requires preparation. It will ask you to look at yourself not as you see in the mirror, but as you hide deep inside the recesses of your being. It will help you shine a light into those nooks and crannies, and open the doors to free the monsters from which you cower in fear. One by one you will confront them, conquering each in turn. As you do, you will construct a new tomorrow from the ground up in which you will thrive. That tomorrow will not have you at the center of its universe. No longer will you see things only in the light of your own self-interest. Instead, you will see yourself a cog in a greater whole, serving your God and all of humanity to build the world of the future. Through your effort on yourself, the world will advance and you will make it a better place for all. But only by your own transformation can it change, one heart, one mind, and one soul at a time.

Most of all, you will find that most precious of substances—love. You will learn to use it, and reflect it in every word and deed of your life. As you do, it will magically melt the walls that separate you from the others in your life. And through your love, you will reshape the world.

Know this well before you start. You do not undertake this journey out of some altruistic sense of service to the world. That would be nice, but that is not its purpose. You undertake the inner voyage for you and you alone. You will do it for the peace it brings you, and the warmth of knowing for the first time in your life why you are here, and what you are called to do. No one can do it for you. The effort must be yours. Patient and persistent must you become, working each moment of every day to weave the lessons later set forth into the fabric of your life.

Come. Find the peace to which you are now a stranger. Map your inner unknown. You will be glad you did.

The Bold Rider

Out of the darkness rode the bold rider
Seeking to find his way to the light
Turning his back on all gone behind him
In search of the truth he rode through the night

First whispers, then cries, he called out for help
Take just a moment to show him the way
Yet try as he might they hid in the shadows
Silently hoping that he would not stay

From door to closed door through town after town
Deaf ears were all turned to drown out his song
The rider undaunted sped through the dark
No map or guidepost to help him along

Though chill of the night cut quick to the bone
His quest's haunting vision bade him go on
E'er forward our rider and gallant steed
Sped seeking the light before it was gone

Alone with his thoughts, no comfort or friends
He longed to return to days past on his mind
And questioned his purpose if no one to share
The gift that was waiting for him to find

Why did they not seek it? Could they not see
The light that awaits to set their hearts free?
What was he missing that others may know
To spurn a taste of the fruit of Life's tree?

He knew in his heart, alone now or not
He could not go back to life without hope
Now that he was freed from Dark's icy grasp
The past was a loss with which he would cope

He wrapped his cloak tighter, kicked in his heels
And urged his great mount to fly with Godspeed
E'en faster they rode, the light near ahead
Its beacon a shelter to all those in need

With a mighty lunge they entered the light
Man and beast joined in triumph as if one
Rays bathed them in peace and washed them in joy
And cleansed them of mem'ries of the night's run

Before he could rest the rider looked back
And saw countless eyes glow faint in the dark
He knew they belonged to those left behind
In hearts where his message had lit a spark

The rider whispered a word to his steed
And without a pause they entered the night
Again wrapped in darkness, the rider returned
To show them the way to bask in the light

The Way of Love

The words I bring you will be easily accepted by some, and totally rejected by others. It is not for me to convince you of the merits of what I speak. This you must do in your own heart, for stored there is the source of all knowledge.

I have passed through many cycles of this experience we call life to shine a light so that others can find their way in the darkness. These past incarnations will not be revealed. Some do not yet believe in the cyclical journey of the soul, and their disbelief should not become an obstacle on the path of awakening as is described here. Let it suffice to say that I lived in various cultures and times, and during those travels I preserved the ancient wisdom and laid the groundwork so that others might follow. Though times have changed, the knowledge has not, for the way to the spirit is the same now as it was then.

Know also that I seek no recognition as a master or one to whom obeisance is given. I experience the same emotions and swings of personality that mark the rest of humanity. Nor do I make any claim of perfection in any pursuit, human or spiritual.

It is for you to decide who I am, and the value to be placed upon these words. For this book is not about me, and must not be judged by my efforts along the path or by my personal characteristics. What I bring is the message of light, and I have gathered here the ancient truths that all must live if they hope to follow the way of the soul and walk the path of awakening.

This mention of past incarnations is of no significance, except perhaps as a point of perspective that the thoughts expressed here may be worth the investment of time and energy necessary to absorb them. Judge their worth for yourself. This is all that will be asked of you. I make no promise or representation that the information here is true, whatever meaning you may assign to that term at this point in your journey. Ultimately, you must decide on the value of the path presented here. For value is always in the heart and mind of the beholder. Only by the weight you assign them will that value be determined.

The comfortable ways of your past may cause these thoughts to rub against you like a burr under a horse's saddle. Or you may find these ideas like an old pair of gloves just waiting for you to slip them on. Either way, any growth or discomfort they bring will be determined by your place upon the path of evolution and readiness for the lessons presented. Whatever you experience, know that the process of your awakening is under way, and will ultimately lead to that for which you long inside.

All that is important is that you are making this journey, testing whether it is time to understand your life in the unfolding story of this world. The answer will tell you whether you will become an active participant in that life, or remain a leaf floating downstream in the great river of time.

Do not go forward with fear or trepidation. Do so instead with a light heart, for you are entering a joyous new tomorrow. Greet the lessons ahead as old friends from whom you have become separated over the years. Allow them to unlock your heart and cultivate your inner being. As they do, permit yourself the luxury of seeing all things harmoniously acting within your sphere, so that you may live in cooperation and not in conflict. To do this, you must learn to love. This book is about the way of love, and how to live it every day. And how love will bring you peace.

We cannot speak of love without also discussing the source of that love, for it is to that source that one day you will return. It is not only the Source of your spirit, but also of all there ever was and all that will ever be. Some may be squeamish to hear of this Source, or uncomfortable to even contemplate its existence. Others are not yet ready to learn and prefer the darkness of their ignorance. If you are among them, try to move beyond the conventions of your comfort to explore the truth of all existence with an open mind.

This source I will speak of as God. Any name can be used, or even no name. It works as well to refer to Him as his nameless creation, the universe. Names are labels assigned by man, and do not define Him. Only He can define Himself, which he does through the totality of his creation.

Jesus called God His father in Heaven. He said God lives in us. And that God is Love.

God the Father. God the Son. God the Holy Spirit. God is one. God is many. And God is all.

God is the Creator of this universe, of all that is seen and unseen. God is the Creator of the planes of existence, and all that is found in each. God is the force and fury and beauty of nature. God is the earth and the skies above. God is the past and the future, folded together in the Now.

God is neither male nor female, but for ease of convention I will use the traditional He—the omnipotent, omniscient Creator. His appearance is unknown. Although we are spiritually in his image, he does not possess the shape or form of these physical bodies. His is not a face we can see.

God just is. Simply and truly, God is consciousness and love eternal. Knowing not limits of time or space or dimensions, God is the Source, the Tao, the way, the truth, and the light.

God is, in His highest and only form, love and light. These are the controlling forces of our universe. These are more than His tools; they are his very essence. God is love, and God is light. Find them, and you will find God.

Mankind craves knowledge about God, in the hope that by knowing about Him, he will know Him. It is not so. Man cannot know God by the words of Man, although the Word as taught by the masters points the way, especially that given by God's manifestation in human form, the Lord Jesus Christ.

To know God, to even find a way of explaining Him and His existence to our own satisfaction, we must each turn inward. Just as we seek to hear the voice of our soul speak through our intuition, we must look inward for God. We may not hear Him. We may not serve his Will. We may not know him at all.

But He is there, ever waiting for us to spread our arms and embrace him, just as any father awaits the return of his prodigal son. Sometimes silent, sometimes whispering, sometimes shouting to get our attention, God is as much a part of us as our own personality. Because God is, we are. Without God, we would not be. Yet without us, God would remain.

God is the hope of our dreams. God is the dream of our hopes. God is all that ever was, and all there ever will be. There is nothing that can be said of God, yet God is all that can be said.

God is love. Love is God. Deny one and you deny the other. Accept one, and you accept the other.

Go with love.

A World Gone Awry

Man has walked the difficult path of civilization for millennia, but still appears to wander aimlessly in the desert. He has little idea where he is, much less where he is going. He rushes headlong in the development of one technological marvel after another, yet grows ever more uneasy with his prowess. Nations vie for power, alternately threatening and unleashing horrific forms of destruction. People fight over differences in their beliefs without considering the merit or choice of those who think otherwise. Worse, too many are without adequate food, shelter, or clothing to gain benefit from the lessons that this life has to offer. What is the point of our great advances if all we do with them is to inflict greater suffering upon our fellow men?

The cycle of violence pervades all aspects of our world. It filters through our entertainment and greets us on the streets. It even hides in the corridors of our schools and shares the comforts of our homes. Few of us can totally escape its reach, or at least its ever-present reminder that menacingly hangs over our heads. Some now fear that our means of violence will soon be exported to the stars, breaking the peace of outer space so we can spread its havoc to other planets and beyond. Is there any hope for us to stay its hand?

Though violence derives as much from attack on our emotional attachments as from fear for our safety and independence, at its core is our egocentric view of life. Our tendency is to think about us first, and judge all by how it affects our interests. We act to protect ourselves lest another may harm whatever we consider our own. Our self-indulgent ways put our own wants at the center of our concerns, causing us to react strongly whenever we perceive their fulfillment is in doubt. If our emotional attachment is strong enough, we respond in the ultimate manner by physically or verbally abusing those who stand in our way.

It is clear that most people live to get what they can for themselves, first grabbing what is needed to survive, and then taking something more to gain an element of satisfaction, comfort, or benefit that the excess can provide. We work and scurry about, trying to grab as much as we can, even if it is more than we need, losing sight that we cannot take it with us at death. In so doing, we callously inflict suffering upon our fellow men who stand in our way.

Our culture has spawned a seemingly endless cycle of greed, producing generation after generation that blindly buys into its egocentric standards. Harder and harder we strive to attain the objects of our desire, yet never do we seem to get enough. It always remains just out of reach, or if attained, is quickly replaced by something new. We are much like the cat chasing its own tail, never catching what we are seeking, and never able to stop.

This egotism is at the heart of our system of government and commerce as well. This pursuit of personal gain is reflected in the rise of capitalism the last two hundred years. Euphemistically known now as commercialism to avoid the competitive stigma that resulted from conflicts between capitalist and communist societies of the 20th Century, the pursuit of profit has spurred tremendous technological achievements. First machines replaced the physical labor of man. Now robotics, miniaturization, computers, and telecommunications have enhanced, and will soon replace, much of our mental and menial work. What do we plan for ourselves when this technological masterpiece is finished?

Though it pretends to be concerned only with the systemic trading of goods and services between nations, at its heart commercialism is fueled by the race for personal benefit. It allows individuals to aggrandize wealth, all under the guise of benefiting the flow of money and growing the world economy. Sanctifying the individual pursuit of desires, this system has brought many accomplishments for society. Unfortunately, it has also created a wide disparity of benefit among individuals.

Our magnificent creation has moved those of energy and vision to great deeds, but all do not share in these works. We have built our society upon greed and hope for personal gain, both shifting sands of social progress that have resulted in much hardship and disparity. Knowledge, wealth, power, and technology are too often amassed in the hands of a few. Some men and even nations gather great wealth and power while others grovel in the dirt for their daily subsistence. These disparities are alarming, fluctuating greatly with life's circumstances, creating significant amounts of social unrest throughout the world, not to mention lives chained to starvation, hardship, and deprivation. Even among the supposed elite some live lives so hollow that they strike out at others in rage and frustration.

Yet our society turns a blind eye to these inequities and the problems they cause, preferring instead to focus on the potential opportunities that are supposedly available to all, provided they have access to sufficient supplies of funds, motivation, connections, and fortuitous luck. The adage, "A rising tide lifts all boats," is often given to justify our blindness to the hardships imposed upon our fellow citizens of the world.

Instead, attention is turned to our marvelous advances in technology, and all of the many wonders it has brought us. Many point to these machines of progress, and say that in them rests our hope for the future. Perhaps hope can come from them, but until directed by a loving heart, it is doubtful their impact will be as great as we pretend.

Nevertheless, even with all our knowledge and technology, we have not attained wisdom. We have failed to move any close to the spirit within us, or to demonstrate the capacity to make love and compassion the centerpiece of our being. The great thinkers upon whose words our civilization and beliefs were constructed never spoke about creating a world where one group was more deserving to receive than another. Yet that is the world we have built. We have a long way to go!

Indeed, man has constructed a great technological masterpiece, but inside that masterpiece is empty. It brings a longer and often-easier life, but it gives that life no greater meaning. It puts the means of communication and information-sharing at our fingertips, but it cannot open our channels to speak with the soul. It is as if man has built a great dwelling, yet put no comforts inside. It has no meaning, no purpose, other than for him to stand outside and admire how nice it looks, while he stands huddled in the cold, bereft of shelter. We must somehow find a way to get inside, and to furnish it to meet the needs of both our inner and outer worlds. If so, we can convert the harsh environment and disparities of today into ones more accommodating and hospitable to the needs of the awakening soul of humanity. Only then can we hope to align our outer actions with the inner values imposed by our souls.

If we are to make these changes, we need a map that will show us how get out of this morass. Such a map is laid before you now in hope that you will choose to travel the inner world to construct a better tomorrow.

Our journey starts with an examination of the reality of our perception. We are here. We live in these bodies. We live in this world. But our examination reveals no reason for our being. It is as if we are mindless pinballs bouncing from obstacle to obstacle. Meaning and purpose elude us when we are caught up in life's events. They flow only from the God that dwells within. Only when we can hear them will we weave our way through the wilderness of this world. With His guidance we will lay the spiritual foundation upon which to construct our lives.

The Creator intended we make this spiritual journey individually of our own free will. Alone we came into this world, and alone we will face our Maker. Motivation comes not from others, but bubbles up from deep within each person's heart. Our good, and that of the world as a whole, depends upon this spiritual transformation, and how these lessons are passed on to future generations. That way is within your grasp. Its map is now laid in your hands in hope that you can follow its clues to awaken your soul. Only through the soul's awakening can you hope to complete your journey of spiritual transformation.

Do not for an instant think that by making this spiritual journey you will be turning your back on the world, or slipping further within the realm of your egotism. Spiritual transformation is not the selfish path of an individual toward his own "salvation." It is instead the pioneering effort of the brave few who dare to venture into the great unknown to blaze a trail for all of humanity to later follow. This inward trek is made single file, one by one passing along the path. One after another we make the journey, each falling in line as our turn arrives. By our efforts, we pull the world a little closer to the light.

The first step is to recognize that our own awakening starts the process for all. As we awaken and share the way with others, they will see the peace and illumination we bring forth into the world, and in turn they too will begin to turn inward. Like a great wave, it will sweep across the land until all are touched and transformed by the simplicity of its message.

Come. Follow me. Let us explore the way together.

A Great Wind is Blowing

There is a great wind blowing. Many have felt it. Some are riding its currents to new awakenings. Alas, some are even using it to their own ends.

We enter the Age of Aquarius, and with it comes a new millennium, a new beginning of sorts. It is a time when the winds of change are blowing out the old and sweeping in the new. Transformation is in the air. It is most striking in the realm of our spiritual belief.

The institutions of our religions are undergoing great tests. They have served their purpose well to stoke the spiritual fires, and have helped their people through their times of strife with promises of life beyond this world. They have taught many rules of right living, but too often they fail to either inspire or show their followers how and why to live those rules at all times. Many profess their faith, but too often that profession is but lip service given for the good feelings they seek and bears little resemblance to the lives they live. As a result, faith is worn on their sleeves, and easily discarded when times get tough. It is little wonder that so few have completed the journey of their souls.

These institutions too often suffer from a misperception of their importance in the spiritual growth of the people, believing that without them none could find the light that flows into this world. Some think that they alone are charged with spreading charity and compassion around the world. They take on many good works, and build vast infrastructures necessary to support them, not trusting that hearts would open to provide needed relief in their absence. As a result, they have developed a mentality that their work must continue above all else, and therefore act to perpetuate their own existence. The resulting inflexibility has built great walls around their beliefs, separating the light from the hearts it is dedicated to serve. These walls have kept men apart, and led to much strife in the world.

A crisis of confidence eats away within these institutions. Many question their church or temple's purity of purpose when its leaders are caught in the material chase or the pursuit of desire. Pay to pray often seems the mantra. Some institutions have used sophisticated means of distributing guilt to aggregate enormous wealth and power in the name of serving their God, causing many to shudder at their worldly ways. Some are even shaken to their core by abuse of their followers' trust. Yet even during times of crisis or questioning, many followers remain motivated by a fire that burns within. Why is this? For what do they hunger? Do they even know?

Still, vast numbers have turned away from the faiths of their fathers. Some look elsewhere for the spiritual sustenance upon which they can grow, moving to another religion and exchanging one dogma for another. Others are alienated by leaders of the temples who have interposed themselves between the people and the source within. Many just drift, cut off from their spiritual roots yet secure knowing that God would not abandon them just because they do not follow a particular set of rules. Still others lose all hope of a world of the spirit beyond this one.

These same problems have plagued us throughout the centuries, for few have been able to live guided by the laws of their faith, much less to complete their spiritual journeys. As a result, mankind has made little spiritual progress since the days the masters openly walked the earth. Even though great churches and philosophies have grown to teach us how to live with each other, we have not learned. Persuasive priests, preachers, rabbis, imams and monks have spoken out in loving tones to reinforce those messages, but as much as we have heard, we still fail to implement the message given by each—that God, or Allah, or Buddha, or whatever name is given to the source of wisdom—is inside us, and there we must look if we hope to find it.

Yes, the word is still spoken, but its truth still has not been absorbed. As much as religions speak of the way, their message is somehow lost upon us. Something is missing, for man as a species lives as if spirit is only for the mystics, and a deity is an all-powerful being that lives in the heavens separate and apart from us. It is time to look beyond the structures and methods of the past, beyond the dogma, and beyond the personalities that teach them, to return to the underlying message the masters had hoped their efforts would spread.

There is no religious component to this teaching. No new spiritual belief is espoused here. This way of light is the completion and fulfillment of that path which you already follow. Whatever your belief, you will not be called upon to leave it behind, but only to challenge it in light of the spiritual truths you learn here. Come from wherever you are, and go to wherever you want. Perhaps you will choose to practice your own beliefs more intensely, with greater faith and passion than you could ever muster before. Or maybe you will find those beliefs do not encompass your newfound growth, and you will discard them as you adopt new practices that reflect the growing influence of the soul in your life. All I promise is that you will be shown the door to the soul, and given the keys to unlock it so you can pass through to the light beyond. But whether you choose to go there is up to you.

Many have already turned their backs upon the structure of traditional teachings of faith, seeking refuge in alternative practices that offer them hope of a better world beyond this one, with methods that are more closely aligned with their beliefs and personalities. Some have even turned to spiritualism, Shamanism, Wicca, and other methods of calling upon the spirit world to tap into that which they know is surely there. But it is not necessary for you to go to such extremes, or to switch to another religion. Do not be too quick to discard your old ways or adopt new ones. The mosque, temple or church you now attend will provide great inspiration and guidance when viewed from the perspective of the lessons of cultivation yet to come in this text, and you will have much to offer those within its faith as your newfound illumination spills out into their world. Use the materials here to supplement what you already have so that they may be well absorbed and adopted before any great changes are made in your life.

Perhaps we can learn from those gratefully known as the masters of the ageless wisdom. They never desired to found great organizations based on strict rules of practice and belief, or to be considered deities in their own rights. Instead, their teachings were intended as indicators of the way to where the spirit dwells, which if followed would allow others to know its peace. Others might have simply used their knowledge to pass through the gate into the world of the spirit. But theirs was a way of service motivated by great love. They took these tools and gave them to every man to use, so that each in turn could follow in his own way.

Throughout the years, many spoke the inner wisdom to all who would listen. Lao Tzu, Moses, Siddhartha, Mohammed, the Pale One—the list goes on and on. They all described a path to truth and a way of life guided from within. While each used different words, they all pointed in the same way—inside—to the source of wisdom, power, and peace of mind, where the answers were waiting to be found. Men did not need to search the outer world for solutions. They only had to look within to find and accept that which was already there.

Even so, their messages fell on deaf ears. Their disciples found the going tough, and the people's ground too hard to accept the seed of their teaching. Many tried, but few succeeded. Men remained as they always were—blinded to the light.

Ultimately, one came who was different from the rest, for he himself was the way and the light. He came as the manifestation of the God that dwells in man, to set an example for us of that which is already ours if we will but find and command it. His name was Jesus. He was called the Christ—the anointed one, the world teacher—who appeared to point the way so that all men might awaken to their light within, and in so awakening find their way back to the source.

Few recognized this Jesus as the Christ, for he did not appear at the head of an army wielding his sword against the enemies of the children of Israel. This Christ was not of the sword, but of the spirit. He was a spiritual warrior, appearing as a reflection of the Creator's love for his creations.

No longer was God the terrible, wrathful, vindictive deity of the Jews. Nor was He the multi-personified gods of the Romans, Greeks, Hindus and others. Jesus taught of a single god that dwelled within. He was a tender and merciful god that opened his arms to all his children and invited them to find their way into his kingdom. Jesus revealed that love was the way to reunify humanity with the Creator who lives within each of us. But even as wonderful as His message was, we have either refused or been unable to follow His guidance to find our way home.

We have not learned these lessons, much less adopted them as our own. We pray without heart. We live without love for most of those around us. And we judge all by the filter of our own desires. We may have listened, but we have not heard. We have taken only what suits us, and left the rest in the temples and churches for when it is convenient to hear.

This all must change. The time has come to go beyond the lessons. The winds of change are blowing strong. The time has arrived for us to become that to which the masters pointed. To do so requires that we set aside our outer ways and seek the God within, becoming the perfect expression of the spiritual beings that we are.

Are you ready?

Sleepwalking

We live in a dream, unaware that all that we see, feel, hear, and touch is a manifestation of our minds. We think we are only that unique package of body, mind, personality, emotions, and ego (in its common parlance) that looks back at us in the mirror each day, and greets the world as we pass by. In our dream, we are supreme rulers of our world, and all creatures big and small bow down to our will.

Most of us give little thought that we may have a soul or spirit lurking somewhere in the body. Even those who do believe such a thing exists give little thought to it during their lives, at least until their survival is threatened. We cannot prove it to the rational satisfaction of our minds, so we do not dwell on it. What point is there thinking about something for which we have no hope of getting an answer, particularly where the alternative is not very pleasant?

We pass through existence without any semblance of an idea of what truly is going on around us. Whether we fail to see the beauties of nature that greet us every day, or tune in to the activities of an unseen world, the fact is that we live in a fog. We are sleepwalking, oblivious to anything other than the dream that occupies us at the moment.

Are we prepared to awaken from the dream and see things as they really are? Or is our reverie so sweet that we cry for another few minutes of bliss, hopeful that a rude awakening will never come?

Cocoon

So long asleep
On this journey through life
Wrapped in the cocoon of my mind
Its shelter a warm respite
From the cold winds of the world without
And the icy unknown within
What is this light
That burns through the walls
Of my fortress
And casts out the shadows of my reverie
Beckoning me to
Awaken from this dream?

Some minds will object to this assertion that life is a dream, and as such is not a true view of "reality" in the physical world, however that concept is defined. To all aspects of their understanding and perception, the world around them is the only existence they have ever known, and there is no rational basis to believe that anything other than that world exists. It is unnecessary to get bogged down in philosophic discussion of the Hindu concept of the great illusion they call *maya*, or whether this physical world exists at all. The concept of dream also encompasses the prospect of altered perception, where life is not seen for all that it is, and that our lack of perception blinds us to its additional possibilities. By undergoing the process I call awakening, we can shift our perception to encompass other things not now within the realm of our awareness.

What can I say to convince you that we are sleepwalking through this life? There are no words that the mind cannot find reason to doubt or explain. It is only the seeking mind that is ready to go forward to see what lies beyond the dream. It is not for me to convince you of the existence of the spirit, or the world that lies beyond our senses. I only suggest that it is so. You must convince yourself, or at least determine to find the answer. Your walk of sleep will not end by itself. If you are to truly awaken to all that is and was and will ever be, then you must choose to find your way out. When you are ready to know, you will begin to look for the answer. If and when you start is up to you.

Once you do, though, sleep's darkness will slowly pass, and you will begin to see. In time you will realize that it is within your power to find the bridge between the worlds. But your awakening will also bring awareness that once you start down the path to that bridge, there is no return. Do not fear the loss of your reverie. When the time comes and the choice is made, you will give up the old ways gladly, and you will not look back.

Until you are ready, you will continue to be seduced by the lure of the dream. It will whisper in your ear, and lull you back into your slumber. It will feed you with desires and will them to life. But when you choose to awaken, the dream will lose its power over you. Once pierced, its veil can never again be pulled over your eyes. You will see through the façade, even if you do not want to.

Do not labor under the misconception that some utopia awaits. The world beyond the dream will not appear as the desiring mind would paint it. Nor will the lifting of its veil replace the sweet fruits of the dream with others of similar reward. In the dream, you sample your desires without remorse. Once gone, they can never again taste as sweet.

I hold out no promise of heaven beyond the dream. All that waits is the soul, and the world of truth, the world of the all. There is great beauty in that world, but there is no way to describe that beauty, for the adjectives of our world of form do not apply. What waits is the spirit in all its glory. It is not of this world. Beyond the dream lies the Source of all to which you will choose to return.

Accord

All that I see and all that I am
Are but an accord
Between my mind and my Self
Born of my refusal
To release the chains
Of this delusion
And return to the source of my creation

Once you see beyond the dream, you will know the nature of the soul, and that it has truly been asleep during your incarnation. You will wonder how you have lived for so long without it, and long for the day it will fully awaken and re-enter your life. You will see the influence of mind in the affairs of men. And you will know the truth about the rules of living set forth by the masters. You will not be able to return, for once awakened, you cannot rebuild your dream. Your sleep will be over, and the time for work upon you.

Once the veil is lifted, you will merely see beyond the façade. You will not yet see the goal, but you will more clearly see the path that you travel. The way remains long, and may seem even longer than before, for your mind has hidden the road to keep you satisfied within its warm confines.

It is not necessary to decide now. You will decide when it is time for you to awaken, to set aside the dream world of your mind and pursue your return to the world of the spirit.

Now is a time for waiting. You have planted the seed of awakening. Soon it will sprout and grow, and with it will come the light of a new beginning. Until then, it waits for the spring to come, to bring water and warmth in preparation for the day it stretches forth toward the sun.

It may not be easy to make such a choice, but you were not born to take the easy way and remain asleep. You were born to walk the path of awakening, and it has never been described as easy. Yet even though the journey is long and sometimes rough, you will know that it is a course that you were born to take. And take it you will, in your own due time.

None but you can sound the call to awaken from the dream. No voice can pierce its veil of silence but your own. I cannot do it for you. I can only point you toward the door, and help you find the keys to it, and to each door in turn through which you must pass. And when you get lost, I will wait for you in the darkness to shine a light upon your way.

But only you can take that walk. When the time is right, you will know whether these words are true. Then, you will decide.

How will you choose?

The Precipice

There is a Divine Plan forged by our Creator that guides our lives as well as the development of this universe. That Plan bids us take this step toward the spirit both individually and collectively as a race of men. It is no longer sufficient to pick and choose those aspects of the Divine Way that we will follow. It is time to act, now!

We are sleepwalking along the edge of a great cliff, oblivious to the danger that lurks below. One false step and we are doomed. And the time for that step is here.

A great hue and cry is spreading throughout the land, "Wake up, mankind. Danger is at hand. Wake up! "

There is no time for delay. The Day of Judgment, as it is known, will soon be upon us. Its wheels are already set in motion!

The time has come for mankind to awaken from its slumber. We must now cross the bridge that we were shown so many centuries ago. This does not mean we must turn our backs on all we have built. The technology of today can work great benefit for all if used properly. But when used improperly, it only perpetuates the great divide that separates the fortunes of men based simply on where and to what circumstance they incarnate.

Throughout the world many have been recently called to explore their own awakenings. Those who can see or hear across the bridge channel messages from masters, angels, and spirit guides, all designed to help us take stock of our lives and awaken to the spirit that cries out to be heard. A renewed public interest is seen where whispers were not before spoken about contact with those who have passed beyond the gate of life. The apparition of the angel of Mary has been seen by countless masses to reawaken man to the need to set aside the ways of mind and will, and seek the spirit that dwells within.[1]

So many have been called because the danger ahead is so great. The masters of our world are sending forth their legions, recruiting them in the battle to save our world and the Plan for humanity's service of the Creator. Some will return to lead men toward this new awakening in hope of averting the coming destiny. Others are preparing the way, gathering the knowledge and shining a light so that others may awaken and begin their own journeys within. More still will assist in the coming years. Each who awakens will serve in his own way. All are serving the Plan.

Make no mistake. It is written that man will turn to the light. But he is given the chance to do it for the sake of what lies within, and not in fear of the fury God's wrath may bring. If man does not heed the call and turn to spirit on his own, then he risks severe hardship. His great accomplishments of mind and will may be sacrificed to drive home the lesson.

These words are not to be taken as specific indicators of havoc to come, for such would only spur fear in mankind. Action must be toward the light, and not away from the danger. Running away from danger reflects fear, which is a negative manifestation of desire—the desire to continue the life of this incarnation, the desire for safety of self and loved ones, or the desire to avoid negative consequences.

Over-emphasis on the danger puts focus on the future, and deprives us of attention to the now. The way to the spirit is through the present. Dwelling on what may or may never come denies us the chance to step into its light. If we are somewhere other than the now, we can never find the door to enlightenment.

Fear of destruction may turn some toward the light. But turning is not enough. All need the strength of purpose and will to see

---

[1] *Fatima Prophecy*, by Ray Stanford. © 1987 Ballantine Books.

it through, and then to return in service of the rest of mankind. Without guidance from the light within, there is little hope that mankind will set aside its foolish ways of mind and will, and turn to the ways of the spirit. Without each man making the journey in turn, the world as we know it will suffer deeply. But then, it has already suffered deeply at the hands of man throughout the centuries past.

The future is not written in stone. We choose our own futures, just as we have chosen our pasts. If we collectively turn within, and live our lives with love and compassion for all, these events will be turned away, and we will set about on the path of new beginning for this earth. If not, the price will be steep. Either way, the world will turn to the light. The mechanism by which it happens is our choice.

Now, at the beginning of this new millennium, is the time to set forth along this path. It is a solitary journey. Although some may make the trip before us, and even shine a light on the way, we must walk the path ourselves. If the goal is to be achieved, it will only be one at a time, each in turn marking the way for the next to follow.

The time is at hand for all men to turn inward and find their light. That is their only hope, and the only hope for mankind.

Breath Break

Take pause
For just a moment
And

Breathe …

Accept congratulations,
For so far you have come
In seeing the world anew
Yet, do not forget to

Breathe …

Now, as you stand upon the precipice
Unsure what to do
Look
To the line of life
That links you
With all of creation, and

Breathe …

Accept this breath
As God's gift
To you
Now and each moment
Of your life

Breathe …

And with each breath
Let flow from you
All fear or concern
Of what may come ahead
Knowing you will meet it
As you have before

Breathe …

Breathe, my friend.
So if nothing more you take
From reading this tome
Let it be to

Breathe …

So when
The tests or lessons
Hiding 'round the bend
Seem more than you can stand
Remember just to

Breathe …

Breathe …

And breathe again …

Whispers in the Darkness

Whispers in the darkness
Haunting through the night
This world we wrap around us
Is not all that is in sight

It lingers in our memories
And tingles in our toes
That more to life awaits us
Beyond the seeds we blindly sow

We know inside that something
More than this must surely be
But fear to stop and listen
To the words that shake life's tree

This world is of our making
It truly isn't real
Created by desires
Of what we want to feel

No matter what our efforts
To stop the maddening voice
It drones on in endless torture
This life is but our choice

A world beyond these bodies
Awaits us ever more
If but we lose our selfish ways
Let truth kick down the door

We think each other separate
From the one that lives inside
And fail to grasp that but one life
In all these bodies hides

The light from which my soul comes
Is just the same as yours
Divided by our bodies' lust
For life's sensory smorgasbord

The voices do not fail us
The path to them is clear
Seek but to find our way out
And the answer will appear

Awakening

Alone

You live in isolation, alone in the world. You see yourself as one, and the rest as the others. It is this way because you do not know who they are, much less yourself.

When you embark upon a course to bring about your own awakening, the boundary between you and the others will slowly begin to dissolve. You will no longer be just you, and they will no more be only others. Part of you will merge into them, and they into you. While your consciousness will still perceive you as apart, it will also begin to recognize that portion of all that is shared.

Why So Hard?

Alone we arrive
And so we leave
Why is the time in between
So hard?

Though you perceive the separateness of the lives you live differentiated by the variances of your bodies, minds, and societal conditions, you are not separate. You are of them, and they are of you. Once awakened, you will no longer be as you now perceive yourself to be. Alone. Apart. One among many. It is only then that you will know that each of you is of the other, as you are of the Source, and the Source is of you.

Nothing more of this can I say now. As enlightenment overtakes you, you will understand.

In the meantime, take solace that you are not the only one who is awakening. Many show its signs, though they may still be unaware. As you will see, those signs are all about you. They are for you to find, and with that recognition choose if and how to respond.

The path is crowded with travelers. Some you must allow to go their own separate way, with nary a hint you know of their journey or that you are on one of your own. Others will need you to shine a light on their way. Still more are simply kindred souls moving toward a shared goal.

Don't expect to neatly categorize everyone who crosses your path. Some will seek destinations that seem quite unlike your own, or try to get there by a path diametrically opposed to yours. Do not let another's way deter you, or fill you with fear or uncertainty. For when the time comes, you will know what to do with what you learn here.

As you venture onto the road ahead, be content simply to look about and know you are not alone. This is a journey all will take, whether they know it or not. It is only your growing awareness that sets you apart.

If you meet others of like purpose and destination, acknowledge and bless their journey. And don't forget to give thanks, for their companionship is a gift to savor along the way.

Until then, enjoy your next step. For that is what it is all about – taking the next step. So what is that step?

To know your own way. And go it with love.

From Dissatisfaction to Despair

There comes a time during some life when we grow dissatisfied with the choices we have made and the lives we have built. Some chalk it up to the mythical midlife crisis, when one naturally examines the course of a life in light of what the future may hold in store. But this can strike at any age, with unrest far greater than unease over work and family issues, questioning the very underpinnings of existence itself.

At first we get only a feeling that things are not as they should be. We continue to go through our daily lives, fighting the same battles of materiality. Efforts to satisfy our desires often increase in hopes that gratification will come from personal indulgences, alcohol, drugs, and sexual activity. Some even devote themselves with even greater vigor to their life's work, hoping that the aggrandizement of power and wealth will fill their needs.

This unease usually will not go away, for it is often the first indication of a soul calling out to the mind that it is ready to begin the process of awakening. Few at this point know it, though, and live life striving harder but getting less from it. They fill their days with one pursuit after another, hoping that the next will finally bring them the peace of mind they are denied. Instead of peace, the unease grows into discontent and then dissatisfaction.

When this happens, the fabric of life is torn by the soul trying to find a way to enter into this plane. The discontent reflects the soul's attack on the façade built by the mind, challenging it to look beyond what is openly visible.

The Ring

I cling to life
Like a ring to a skeleton's finger
Dangling
By a thread frayed
Over the precipice of uncertainty
Awaiting a breath
That might never come
In a tomorrow that may never be

I long to breathe the air
That will flow anew in that time not now
Desperately clinging to
the hope of another day
Or life
That is but a distant dream

If but I knew my end was near
What deed would be my last?
What would I say? Who would I have hear?
Would a river of words flow
From this voice so often dammed?
Or my heart swoon to the song of another's soul
I may never touch again?

Each day brings struggles
For things I'll leave behind
A sprint to a false reward
Like a ghost in the fog
Now here then gone
In this world
Where spirits ride their ships of flesh
Sailing silently into the night

Cynicism often prevails as the mind gains awareness that the world is not as it seems, and commonplace activities now are filled with subterfuge and intrigue. The mind doesn't know yet to look behind the façade, so it evaluates the world on the terms it always has. It sees injustice, but cannot see further so it attributes it to the selfish motives of those involved. Without an answer to its growing cynicism, the discontented mind seeks to escape, but cannot find the way out.

The mind becomes sick as it is overcome by the longing remotely imposed by the soul. The uneasiness trickles into the emotions, and influences the physical body to manifest a variety of physical ailments generally referred to as dis-ease (it is not to be presumed that these preliminary feelers of the soul are the cause of all disease, since the physical body is susceptible to unbalance by many influences, including invasion by bacteria and virus, injury, and etheric imbalance, among others).

Ultimately, the mind pushes the emotional body into depression. As it moves deeper into the darkness, the mind becomes more desperate for an answer to its dissatisfaction. It despairs in its inability to control either the emotional or physical reactions to what still remains an unidentified attack on its reverie. The puzzle of life is now a maze, without escape or satisfaction.

This is a crucial time of incarnation. Unable to turn their backs on the "madness" of the world, some give in and throw up their hands in frustration. Others sink into the pit of insanity, their minds racing here then there, searching for a way out yet not seeing the door that stares them in the face. Others commit suicide, ending this incarnation and hopefully leaving the whole mess behind.

Life at this point is painful, to say the least. The emotions run strong, objecting to the mind's inability to focus and interfere with its normal functioning.

However, those who persevere through the darkness begin to see a light in the distance. At first nothing more than a pinpoint, as they move closer it begins to come into form. Slowly it changes into the shape of a person, still too faint to make out. So they continue on. The light grows brighter. The shape grows clearer. The image they see is none other than themselves, reflected by the mirror of their soul. The light illuminates them so that the reflection once hidden can now be seen.

Amazed, the man begins to look at himself from the outside. No longer caught up in the emotions and thoughts of the moment, he moves beyond his despair to a point of reference outside his body. Suddenly he is the watcher, silently observing that which he thought he was all along. Totally immersed, he is awestruck by the totality of his essence.

It is at this moment that the feelings of discontent fall by the wayside, replaced now by wonder at this magnificent creature that stands before his eyes. Even through the bewilderment, it is like nothing he has ever seen before. At once simple and complex, he sees the thoughts swirling about the body's axis. He also takes note of the emotions that pulsate rhythmically inward and outward until they suddenly explode, and then just as quickly recede.

Amazed, he looks again. How could he be this being that is reflected before him? How could he have missed all of this before?

But then he wonders the most important questions of all. What's it all about? Why am I here?

All Within Reach

In the zenith of my life
With all that I can desire within my reach
The safety of my nest is lost
A crack through which the light of the soul
Does shine
Beckoning me to stop
And ask myself
Why?
How can I awaken from this dream?

The Quest

To ease his dissatisfaction, the pre-awakening man asks, "Why do I feel like this? Is there something more to life?" Yet those around him tell him to quit acting strange and get on with his work. Society tells us that life's purpose is to get up and work and go home to sleep and get up to do it again. Once we provide for our survival, it dangles the carrot by allowing us to try to get a little something more for us. Something inside cries out that there is more to life than this.

Some realize that they don't have the answers, and must find them if they are to have peace of mind. They begin looking, turning to one promise after another. Sometimes they find solace in what is shown to them. Most of the time, though, their disappointment grows as it fails to stop the voices running inside their heads, or it just "doesn't feel right" to them. So they look some more, bouncing from one method to another, hoping that one of them will take control and tell them what to do in order that they can again be satisfied. Many fall prey to cults and esoteric fringe religions, or adopt unusual philosophies of charismatic leaders that espouse dogma that promises to soothe their confused minds. Desperate for relief, they gladly seek shelter within its embrace, blind to the fact they are simply exchanging one façade for another as the mind seeks to regain control. The despair will soon return, but the chains of their new attachment will be even harder to break before they can again be on their quest.

Others concoct their own version of "wisdom soup," taking a little of this and a little of that to suit their fancy. Under this pinball approach, they recognize no absolutes. Truth becomes relative – whatever fills the void is okay.

In one sense, that may be true. The mind is so distraught that anything that gives it order brings relief. In the eyes of a material world, peace of mind comes with an orderly structure of beliefs. Such order brings with it the opportunity to again gain control of mind and return to a life of will and desire. Since mind, through its manifestations of will and desire, is the predominant force moving our society, such a synthesis of beliefs meshes well, so long as it allows the mind to return to the accepted ways of thought and deed.

Unfortunately, while there are many truths hidden among the various paths, those adopting a spiritual smorgasbord approach usually fall prey to the same problem experienced among the world's religions. That is, both the spiritual explorer and the religious traditionalist fail to go beyond the structure or words and truly take the lessons to heart and apply them to life.

Nevertheless, such "spiritual relativism" does touch upon one important fact – the seeking mind looks all around for answers, yet cannot find them. It may find pieces of what it thinks are answers, but these pieces don't fit the puzzle of the mind. The mind believes there is an answer to its growing madness, and that this madness somehow relates to that which is beyond comprehension in worldly terms. So the spiritual search goes on in an accelerating spiral into the darkness, blinded to the fact its own soul is hastening the descent.

Piece by piece the soul tears away the mask the mind has worn for so long. Understanding, purpose, and even its reason for being now seem beyond grasp as the mind clutches for certainty like a drowning man does for a lifeline. The rational mind longs to turn back and find another mask, but the soul continues its incessant onslaught. It whispers in the ear of mind, "Wake up. Wake up." And slowly the slumbering mind begins to awaken to the calling soul. With that awakening comes a glimpse of an outer world that is but an expression of the spiritual foundations beneath it. Though the outer mind still can't escape its need to dominate its environment, it begins to notice little things that were previously obscure. Under this new light, it uncovers hints of meaning and patterns behind what once appeared as random events.

Grasping for order and meaning, the mind begins a process of observation. It looks around and notices that information seems to appear just when needed, or that chance meetings or events bring needed relationships. The mind looks back over its incarnation, and notices the conflux of seemingly unrelated happenings that shaped the life it knows today. Insignificant decisions, and even life's travails, may have even set the stage for some later major occurrence far down the path of life.

Once written off as coincidence, the inquiring mind begins to wonder. Is there in fact such a thing as coincidence? Or, is it the result of some plan? How could all of these events happen by chance, when some (no matter how small) have put us in position for the significant moments of our lives? But if there is such a plan, whose is it? And who is it that arranges things to turn out the way they do?

So many questions. So much uncertainty. We do not yet realize that nothing in our lives is certain, each experience being shaped by the choices that came before. Even those choices, though, do little to prepare us for the realizations to come.

The only certainty for those who walk this earth is that some day their bodies will die. All are left to wonder whether their consciousness, or any part of them, will live beyond that event.

Many, coming from religious backgrounds, speak of a life after the death of these bodies. Buddhism teaches that we live life after life of suffering, from which cycle we can be freed by achieving enlightenment through right living on the middle path. Christianity teaches that man can achieve "salvation" if he allows love to guide his life and relationships with all, recognize and repent his wrongs, and believe in Jesus as the way to such life. Still others follow a myriad of methods, but most hold out the hope that there is benefit to "right living," and a life beyond that which we know.

Are these just codes of social conduct, or truly paths of spiritual development?

Man is uncertain what happens after the death of his body, yet most people harbor the hope, and in some a "mindless" belief (for such a belief cannot come from mind, which has no knowledge or experience upon which to base it), that life somehow extends beyond the grave. Man's mind wants to believe the teachings, but part of it holds him back. This duality wages a war inside him. Will he live, or will he not? Life is lived trying to block out such thoughts, yet the mind always has one eye on the grave, wondering what if anything lies ahead.

Most of us choose to live our lives in the only world that we "know" is for sure – the touchy-feely world of this dimension. We think we know that the earth and water that we see, the air that we breathe, and the people we encounter, are all "real." Everything else is a promise of something more. Since our minds seek justification and gratification, it is indeed difficult to live for promises. Behavior and belief are therefore only partially shaped by the rules of right living, as we will call the standards of behavior promulgated by religion.

Why Do I Believe?

Why do I believe
In life beyond
The days of my flesh?
If I'm right and how I live
Determines life beyond
Then that alone should be enough
To keep me living right
But if I'm wrong and this is all
No more days beyond my breath
Then why not do it right
Since ne'er again shall I have this chance?

Belief in the hereafter is taken skeptically, some accepting it more than others, so that the rules of living are followed to the extent convenient within the mind's view of this three-dimensional world.

Even given the underlying skepticism that inflicts most of mankind, the inquiring mind truly wants to know more. Its observation of life leads it to examine this concept of continuity of life, and to explore phenomena that suggest it is more than a theory.

The inquiring mind also begins to explore phenomena once hidden from public view and only spoken of in hushed terms. Psychics interpret the vibrations of our energy fields, and mediums transmit messages received from images of the departed who have passed into the next world. Clairvoyants see the future. Many ordinary people not even claiming such powers experience contact with those to whom some refer as apparitions or ghosts. Magic, witchcraft, and voodoo all practice "dark arts" to call upon spirits in another world to do their bidding.

It is difficult for the mind to accept such phenomena without rational explanation, so it attempts to deny their legitimacy. Nevertheless, after a period of despair, even the disbelieving mind will examine these things, hoping to find a clue to the source and cure of its "disease." They suggest that "life" may not necessarily be what we think it is, and that what we see is not all there is.

The inquiring mind examines these phenomena, trying to come up with a good reason to explain them. It craves to re-establish order in its universe ruled by mind and will. These events dash cold water on its efforts, pointing out once again the anomalies in the facade that it created. There is something more. It must find out what that is. The quest goes on.

That something is the esoteric foundation underlying all of existence, the world hidden from the view of our senses. That something is the world of the soul. Many do not believe in the soul. Our purpose is not to debate that point, nor to convince you that there is such a thing or even whether it outlives the body. Our concern is to understand its role in our discontent, and find a way to awaken it to guide our lives in this world

Jesus taught us to seek and we will find. He knew that we could not find our answers in the world outside. Yet he knew we had to look, for only after we looked without success would we be willing to explore the unknown ground within.

Now it is time to begin the quest in earnest by looking within, to find what we already know and have locked deep inside. The hardest thing to accept on the path of awakening is that we already know the answers, and that they are just waiting for us to discover that which is already ours. We struggle with this concept, and continue to look around, hoping against hope we can find them anywhere but in this morass of thoughts and emotions we know ourselves to be. Yet no matter how hard we look, we cannot find the answers we seek. Exhausted, we finally give up, and turn to a power beyond the selves we know for answers. We open the door to the soul, and plead, "Teach me." And the next phase of our journey begins.

Giving Up — And Giving In

There comes a time in the search when we realize that we cannot attain what we seek through mind and will. Mind may conceive and will it to come true, but that alone does not insure the way of the spirit will be ours.

The frustration and sense of impotence becomes overwhelming. Here we seek the answers to life's questions, yet we are denied not only the answers but also any semblance of what little peace we may have known before. Worse, there is no return, for now the awareness has started, showing us that there is something more, and denying us the sweet taste of the simple pleasures of desire upon which we once feasted.

Life at this point is not fun. It does not satiate the desire that still lives within us. It is simply seeking. We walk the path of awakening, but know not its attainment. We have burned the bridges behind us, but the way ahead is not yet revealed. Fear of the unknown overtakes us, and we often stumble, reverting to the old ways of emotion and desire, then beating ourselves up for allowing them to overtake us.

Fear

Fear
Reduces even the bravest soul
To a trembling fool
Cowering
In the night

Finally we fall flat on our faces. Unable to stand, unable to go back, and unable to go forward, we throw ourselves at the mercy of the as-of-yet unknown and unseen God that waits for us within. "Master," we cry, "Help us. Show us the way." Yet He says nothing. Why? Why? Why??????

The problem is that the mind has not given up its attempt to control all within its reach. Its will still paves the way, and its desire marks the ground behind. Eventually, though, it gives up the need to have things its own way, and quits asking, "Why?" Quietly sobbing, we prostrate ourselves and cry, "Do with me what you will. What I want is not important. Make me the instrument of your will. Thy will be done."

We become the ultimate sacrifice to our quest. Unable to go back, and unable to go forward, we offer ourselves up to His fiery Will. We burn the world of our minds on the altar of God. And so we die, preparing to be reborn.

Sacrifice

Take me, my God
And play this instrument of my soul
In the symphony of Thy Purpose
That its sweet tune
May all the Heavens bless
With haunting melody

Thy gift in trust
Of all I am or ever hope to be
I lay upon the altar of your Word
For without it so hollow rings this life
That to use it on my own
I care not even to try.

Out of the ashes the Phoenix did rise. And from the ashes of our own sacrifice, the door blocking the way to the soul will open. The messages will come, if we will but listen. God's light will shine. And love will begin to light our way, and shine on all whose lives we touch.

This is the ultimate step in our preparation to truly hear the intuition and awaken the soul. It is the spiritual aspirant's rebirth into a life of discipleship, to study at the feet of the inner Master himself, and to serve Him in all aspects of life. Now the desperation of the seeker is gone. He is filled with hope and warmth and the beginnings of the wisdom that tapping into the God within will bring. He has his first inkling of purpose for his being. And as he has learned, so will we.

To walk the path of attainment we must give up and give in. The sooner this happens, the sooner we will begin to uncover the true understanding that already hides within.

Sacrifice yourself unto God. Deliver yourself to Him, and He will deliver to you all of the glories and power of the Kingdom of God, not just for your own benefit, but to serve all of mankind. So spoke Jesus. So is the Way. And so it is.

Jesus sacrificed himself to serve the will of God. And so must we all, for his death was the call to arms for each of us to follow. The teachings of many religions do not recognize that Jesus was the son of man, sent by God as the Messiah to lead his people out of the darkness. They do not recognize that he was killed and then rose from the dead to again lead his followers toward the light. But all believe that this Jesus was a prince of peace, who gave up his life for his belief in the supremacy of his god. All believe that Jesus sacrificed himself in furtherance of the Divine Will revealed to him.

We, too, must be willing to give up everything, even our lives, to serve God's Plan. Only then will we be permitted to move forward with our preparations. Only then will we be worthy of the gift of knowledge and love that He has hidden within us.

We prepare not for our own individual benefit. We prepare only so that our souls can act through us in this world so that we may do our part in furtherance of the Divine Plan.

What sacrifice is too great to gain entrance into the kingdom of heaven? What sacrifice is too great to deny yourself the chance to experience nirvana in this lifetime? Is there anything that you would withhold as sacred?

If so, then you are not ready. If not, what are you waiting for?

*fear
of death
stalks us all
silently watching,
waiting for us to blink
when we look mortality in the eye
so it can take its icy grip around our minds*

Fear and Hope

*hope springs eternal when we consider what
happens when our breath last leaves
these frail bodies and souls are
freed from fleshly chains
to go whence we do
once this life
is over*

Seek What the Master Sought

Seek not to follow in the master's footsteps. Seek what the master sought. So many want to follow the ways of their teachers. "Do as I say or do," they are taught. Inherently they are limited by their master's knowledge and skill of teaching, for by doing what the master does, without the intent of the master, is useless. If one seeks to walk in the master's footsteps, one will learn to follow footsteps. But if one seeks some higher goal, then one will ultimately attain that higher goal.

The true seeker does not blindly follow the master that went before. Instead, he uses his master as a beacon, and forges ahead as his master holds the light high to illuminate the path. But always he seeks the source of that light, not the master. And once he finds it, points the way for others who follow. The true master is a seeker that has walked a little farther down the path, motivated inwardly by his quest for light. When he finds it, he shouts to the rest, "Here it is. Come see." But only those who also seek the light can find it. Otherwise, they find only his footsteps, and the taunting whispers of the wonders they miss.

Seek and you shall find. Those who look for the light will find it. Those who do not look can never find it. This is the way. But looking is not merely watching through life's window at whatever happens to pass by, in hope that it will suddenly appear out of magic. To find, looking needs an intention to find forged from strength of purpose that will keep us going when darkness surrounds us and we fear we've lost our way. It does not always seem this easy. Some look and give up. The truth is to seek. Not to seek for a while, but to seek all of the time with all of one's heart, mind, and especially soul. With this, then one will find. There is no other way.

Looking is not enough. Seeking focuses the power of creation to manifest that upon which the desire is focused. Seek. Find. In ways of the spirit, one will not occur without the other. For the soul wants to be found. It cries out for us to awaken, so it can assert itself once again in our lives, to rejoin with its lower selves and to serve its master in this world.

Seeking requires us to be willing to learn and do whatever it takes to step into the light. We must be willing to not only find the answers, but to apply them to ourselves. We must use them to completely transform mind, body, and emotions into a unified instrument played by the soul.

Seeking means being willing to follow the map that is revealed to us as we look for each milestone. Find it. Uncover its secrets. Learn its hints of the next one that lies ahead. Onward and inward we go, gradually bringing more and more light into our lives. Looking, though, is not enough. Each milestone requires us to act upon the knowledge it brings. Knowledge about what we are, and what we must do to move forward. But the next milestone will not be revealed until we learn the lesson of the one before. We must implement that knowledge as we travel. The milestones give us feedback of how well we have done that, and what next lies ahead.

However, too many want to seek, but do not want to change. They want to gather knowledge as a form of personal satisfaction, a reflection of their desires and insecure belief that being no better than the others is not enough. The search for wisdom is their way of setting themselves apart, not joining closer. It says, "Hey, look at me." Many may start on this course, but those who are not ready to apply the lessons will soon become disheartened and quit.

There is nothing in the search for the "me" of desire. Without gratification for the ego, the quest soon loses its meaning. Those who are not willing to change will fall by the wayside, perhaps to try again in another incarnation, perhaps never to try at all, at least until the flower of desire[2] withers and is ripped from their hearts.

Seeking must be for the sole purpose of joining with the spirit, and bringing its light into our lives. Seeking is the search to find God who dwells within, and to say to Him, "Take me, I'm yours."

To the true aspirant, I say, "Fear not. You will find your way. The road may be long, and the way unsteady, but each step will bring you greater light, and the gift of love awaits your arrival."

To the semi-casual seeker, wanting only to awaken intuition to get more guidance and fulfillment out of life, I say, "Walk a while and listen. Hear the voice whisper? Walk just a while farther, and its voice will become clearer. With each step you can better hear its tune – so beautiful and so warming to the soul. If you tire, rest a while, then come a little closer."

And to he whose heart is filled with desire, where mind and will rule and his search is but an inquisitive venture into the unknown, I say, "You must use both hands to open the door, and venture to the wonders that wait beyond. Put down your burden. It is so heavy anyway. You will not miss it here. And if you choose, you may always return for it later. For now, step inside, and rest from the ravages of the outer world."

Come. Join us. Find what you have been looking for. It waits for you inside. Let me show you the way.

---

[2]Mabel Collins, *Light on the Path* (1888, 1911). Reprinted Kessinger Publishing Company (September 1997)

Why Me?

The soul. So much has been written about it throughout the ages that further discussion seems unnecessary, if not futile. Nevertheless, perhaps a different perspective will help.

Your soul's unanswered call is your source of discontent, sent forth by its need for you to invite its force into your life. It whispers that you are not all you can be, and bids you to undertake a journey to awaken its influence in your life. Yet awakening is not an event of sudden enlightenment or realization like the Japanese concept of *satori*. It is more of a process, a path that must be traveled. Though changes occur with each step, the final transformation is more gradual, like that of a flower seen opening under time-lapse photography, incomplete until the flower of the soul has fully bloomed in the world of form.

Once underway, awakening does more than transform the mind and body into a vehicle for direction by the soul. It is a two way street. The mind relinquishes its will to serve the soul, inviting it to act through it in the tangible world of form. And when fully awakened, the mind draws upon the soul's powers and focuses them in its service of the Divine Plan.

You already walk the path of awakening, though you may not know it. It is a process that starts with your first life, and continues through your last. Your discontent is just a sign that the time is near for you to do so in earnest. The soul is inviting you to become aware of your travel, and focus your efforts so you can overcome the pitfalls that so often crop up as we gather experiences along the way.

Even as your awareness brings you a glimpse what you must do, something holds you back. What is it that you see in the distant fog? What are these obstacles that seem so great? How will you ever get around them? As you grow closer, you see that they are not mountains to climb or rivers to cross. You see that they are far more than something you can surmount by hitching up your pants and strengthening your determination. No, worse, they are reflections of that which is within you, the hardest things of all to overcome. Yet your soul calls you to take them on one by one on your journey ever inward.

No matter how true you know this calling to be, you are still a creature of mind and emotion, and must overcome their resistance if you are to embark on this inner journey. Over and over they whisper their objections in your ear. "Why you?" they ask. "Can't things stay the way they are? Must you make this journey? What is in it for you?" And so you begin to wonder, "Why me?"

The answer may be difficult to hear. There is nothing to assuage the ego in the search for inner knowing. There is nothing to stroke the personality by awakening the soul. There is nothing to satisfy your desire. In fact, there is nothing in this path that will feed, much less satisfy, any personal hunger for wealth, power, fame, recognition, love, or whatever. Only the subordination of desire, the subjugation of ego, and the submission of the personality's extremes lie ahead. Who would undertake such a rigorous course just to get a glimpse of the life that dwells within each of us? Don't they bring us the joys we get from life? Why is it so important for us to know?

Our great discontent with this life stokes the fire of our curiosity. We know there must be more than what we see, and like the great pioneers who braved the unknown frontier "just because it was there," we are willing to venture forth from our places of comfort to explore of the inner world just because we now know it is there. And maybe, just maybe, we will be allowed to savor the sweet taste of illumination that we may find along the way.

What is it that hides behind the veil of our awareness? What is this life that dwells within us? What is this thing called spirit or soul, and why is it so important to us?

At the heart of these questions is the mystery of life itself. Man's attempt to grasp its magnitude has pitted science's attempt to explain the phenomenal world against religion's faith. Each tries to explain a complex biological process that magically produces a new, living creation imbued with consciousness, identity, and the will to survive in a divine mystery known only to the Creator. We hope that better understanding of this soul will perhaps bring greater knowledge of us and our reason for being. It was this life that the masters sought to know. This was the reason for their journey within, and this is the reason why you must make it now.

The masters sought the inner world to learn the secrets of life itself, to find that same meaning we all long to know. They were no different from you and me in their motives. Only in their means did they differ, for they accepted and took to heart those very lessons here set forth until they became a part of their lives and very being. They took those lessons and lived, ate and breathed them until they seeped into their sinews and filled every pore. Those lessons are laid before you here, baring the secrets of the ageless wisdom that have been passed down in so many forms throughout the years.

Before those secrets were revealed, the masters had to learn the true nature of the life that dwells within man. There was no other way. Their inner longings told them something greater lay in store if they could but pierce the armor of their fleshly shell. These same longings cry out within you as well.

Do you hear their call?

The Nature of Man

A Story of Creation

"In the beginning was the Word, and the Word was with God, and the Word was God."[3] And so life began. From that union sprang the form from whence came all of creation. So it was, and so it is.

The Bible teaches that God created man in his image. So many assume that image to be the physical form of these human bodies, yet though we see that form, we do not know God. For God gave man no glimpse of Him, and similarly concealed from man the very image that He created. All that remained was the shell that we know as the body of man.

Man has labored throughout his existence over this fact, knowing only what he could see, and then even guessing about that. Somehow the masters were able to see beyond the shell. How did they do this? What did they learn?

John's verse guides all who seek the inner domain, for it hides the key to unlock the door to their inner temple. Many have interpreted his use of "the Word" to mean that Jesus was with God from the beginning. But it was not God that John extolled in this passage, nor Jesus either, but a power that existed separate from, yet as a part of, the deity of God Himself.

The human mind has enough difficulty fathoming the existence of God Himself without trying to conceive of an omnipotent force that existed before, with and through Him. Yet here John begins his opening lines by telling us that this power he called the Word was present from the beginning; it existed with and was God. It

[3] John 1:1

expressed its absolute intelligence and power by creating life, and through that life, bringing light to the darkness. Why was it so important that John give homage, first and foremost, to the power of the Word, and not to the God that wields it? What was it that commanded his awe even greater than God, the almighty deity Himself, or the son of light of whom he taught? Perhaps we can gather some insight from the words themselves.

Words express intelligence put to action through intent. Here the Word refers to an active intelligence of unlimited power and scope that existed before God. This intelligent unlimited energy formed the intent to know itself, and in so doing, took its identity as God. This energy, this active intelligence that John called the Word, became God, and through that identity wielded the power and might of the Divine active intelligence. It is this active and absolute energy of intelligence behind all of creation that John described and to which he paid homage. It is this, the master intelligence and absolute power that is the source about which John tried to teach us, and which Jesus came to illuminate. The spark of this power to which John gives his obedience is expressed through our soul, the god-power within us.

Once this intelligence became aware of its identity as God, it discovered that its expression was limited, for there was nothing against which to compare its existence. There was no mirror, no others, no light, no darkness – it was all that was. Determined to know itself further, it conceived a Plan of self-exploration by which to reflect all its aspects. Now manifested in its identity as God, it poured its power into this Plan expressing His Divine intent, and brought forth what we know as the creation. He called out the sacred word of the universe, the cosmic AUM, which caused His essence to differentiate and separate itself into various units of consciousness, each a part of the other as much as a part of the one from which it came. Each unit was a self-contained aspect of the Divine One, holding within it the three-fold spirit – spiritual will, consciousness, and active intelligence. Each shared a part of the Creator's energy, and reflected His will to know and experience itself and the rest of His creation. Through consciousness it carried awareness of itself, and through its active intelligence applied that will and knowledge to fulfill its purpose. Each unit, or spirit, was an aspect of His divine essence, bearing a spark of the Word from which it sprang. Each spark was a point of light within the greater Light of the Creator. These points of light were sent forth to carry out different parts of His Plan so that He might know and experience himself through all aspects of the existence He created.

His Plan was that light would shine through the darkness, expressing itself through love as it interacted with the other aspects of Himself that He created. Each spirit would play a different role while gathering experiences to become part of His One Experience, and then after serving its role, return to the Source. Though lesser in degree, each spirit was a mirror of God Himself, and given the opportunity to know itself in all its facets so that it could choose how to travel the great path of return to the light from the darkness of separation.

God realized that He could not fully experience His plan of love and light without also creating the seeds of darkness against which to contrast the experience of light, and to provide each spirit the choice and means to return home. And so he created the world of form into which His different aspects were permitted to pass and become a part, so that they too could experience the fullness of their being. So each spirit was empowered to construct a soul through which it could direct its will and intelligence in the world of form to perform its unique role within His Plan. This soul linked each spirit with the world of form, where it could begin to know itself through the arduous process of gathering diverse physical, mental and emotional experiences over many cycles of lives. In effect, the soul was a transformer that "stepped down" the God-power allocated to the threefold spirit so it could enter and experience this physical world.

These spirits entered the world through all aspects of form, including plant, animal, mineral, and even the planets themselves. Some even took on that most special role as human beings with the power of thought, expression, and responsiveness to better gather these experiences. It was through this creation of man that God could most effectively know himself.

However, the seeds of the spirit's undoing were planted when the mind was linked to the physical body through an intermediate layer of emotions. This layer we will call the desire body, for through this emotional aspect flowed the spirit's desire to incarnate, thereby establishing in each physical being the will to live, and to insure its survival. However, once desire was superimposed on the lower mind, other desires overcame and enslaved the mind and physical body. The emotions soon became dominant, and swung wildly in response to the attainment or denial of desire. Desires quickly pushed out all vestiges of higher purpose as they preoccupied the mind with the search for sensation. As a result, man lives enslaved to desire – mind and body, sandwiched around emotions, all estranged from the soul that gives them life and meaning for existence. It is this sleeping, ignorant, desire-infested man who rules the earth in pursuit of his own gratification. Man has wrapped himself in the darkness, unaware of the light from which his spirit was birthed, and that shines through his soul. It is this man whose soul pleads for him to escape the chains of his bondage.

Man was given the power of choice so he could return to the Source, and in so doing overcome the call of his desires. Man's choice so far has been to turn closer to those desires, thereby living in denial of any purpose other than his own survival and gratification. Through ignorance he turns away from the light and dives deeper into the darkness. The time has come to restore the Plan, and let love and light shine in the tangible world. Only then can man finally know God, and through man's experience, God can know Himself. And in so doing, begin our long trek home.

Journey to the Soul

Man is more than the composite of his mind, emotion, and physical body. Man is above all a spiritual being that asserts its will through the soul. These aspects with which we face the world are nothing without the soul. Yet we know nothing of our spiritual roots.

The soul gives meaning to life. It links us with our Creator through the spirit, own personal aspect of the light. It is the Christ within us, and shines the light that guides our lives. It gives us our quality of being, bringing consciousness into bodies that would otherwise be nothing more than shells animated by the breath of life. The soul is all of these and more.

With a life that exists beyond that of our physical bodies, the spirit is said to live for all time. In a sense this is true, for time itself is a manifestation of the physical universe, and the spirit exists beyond its realm. The events of today are but folds overlapping on all the yesterdays and tomorrows throughout time. The spirit was then, is now, and will be when time runs out. It lives through the soul in the now, no matter when that may be. Those in unity with the soul will see beyond the "reality" of this world and time will fold back upon itself. Past and future will be revealed.

The soul cannot be found in these words. It cannot be found in the halls of man's learning. It cannot be found in the temples, or the wonders of nature that surround us. Yet, its image is reflected through all of these.

Our true nature is consciousness divided. Dominated by our lower minds, we are estranged from our higher selves, sleepwalking without awareness of our higher beings. We retain only an uneasy longing that provides but the hint of something more. Like a twin separated from its birth mate, we feel empty inside, without apparent reason or rhyme for our discontent. A piece is missing, and we are compelled to find it. For our soul requires wholeness. It craves to be one with its lower parts, and calls them to awaken. It pleads for unification, and beckons us to cross the unknown frontier and pass through the gate to its world.

Knowing that it calls to us presents us with something of a dilemma. Like an estranged twin, we are anxious to meet our other half. Unfortunately, our fervent desire is not enough to make it happen. We cannot simply jump from where we are to where we must go through some exercise of magic or change in perspective. We are unprepared to face the soul. Without this preparation we will never reach the door that separates our worlds, much less pass through. Only through our personal transformation can we demonstrate our readiness for contact with the Divine.

Change. Transformation. Something about these words is disturbing. Their very sound attacks our serenity. They imply we are insufficient the way we are, and worse, ask us to set aside the known comforts of who we are and the lives we live in hope of attaining something more. Faced with such a choice, is it any wonder that so many of us want to remain asleep, snuggly wrapped in our blankets of darkness? What we end up with may not be better than what we have, much less what we are seeking. It is hard to face our fear of the unknown, much less choose to travel such a difficult road in search of an unknown soul. But when it comes down to it, few look for this awakening. Instead, the journey is thrust upon us, rudely turning us out of the warmth of our known worlds.

Yet why should this call to change be a cause for concern? The only certainty in your life until now was change, for its hand has shaped each moment from your first breath until now. You have been making this journey your entire life. The only difference is now you will do it with your eyes wide open, consciously treading each step along the way. Knowing that each is an experience gathered on the journey of your soul.

Look where you are. Isn't that place hollow and without joy so much of the time? Has life dealt you such a wonderful hand that you do not wonder why it has unfolded this way, or where it will go from here? Or most of all, do you withdraw from the pains it has inflicted, hoping against hope the knife that caused them will never be wielded again? Is this so very much to leave behind?

You don't need anyone to convince you of the merit. This is a trip you want to make; it is one you have to make. And you will do so gladly, embracing the exhilaration of being born into the world anew.

Do not think you are not ready. You need no supplies. You need no special education or training. Everything needed you will find along the way.

Neither should you be concerned that you travel alone. We each become aware at different times and places. Even when you meet others who also journey to the light, do not be concerned about their speed or apparent place along the way. Each of us progresses at our own rate.

Cast out all fear of failure. For you cannot fail. The path is wide, and grows wider with every step you take. Just your very act of trying insures your success. Your soul will not allow you to fail. When you fall, it will whisper for you to get up, and give you strength to go on. As it is written, so it is now and will always be – seek and you shall find. Therefore build your world with a light heart and joyous attitude. Be grateful for all you experience along the way, for these moments are your reason for being.

The outer mind's impatience may carry over to this inner journey. There is no magic wand to waive that it be completed overnight. This inner transformation cannot be rushed. Though passage is guaranteed, it may not always be steady, or occur within the time frames you desire. Sometimes the going will not be so swift, nor will progress come as easily. Early successes may raise expectations to replicate the speed of earlier gains. You may hunger to again taste the feeling of accomplishment. If you don't, frustration and doubt will set in as your impatience grows. These are the reactions of a mind seized upon a goal, wanting to rush ahead to its completion.

Sometimes you will need to catch your breath and appreciate the experiences gathered along the way. That may mean taking a step backward to regain that which you discarded or felt was too insignificant with which to bother. Use such moments as refueling stops to prepare you for the work ahead. Strengthen your resolve to see through your course, and cultivate your ability to wait, for this is not a race that goes to the swift or the strong.

You cannot force the changes you now so ardently desire. You cannot compel the soul to awaken. You cannot summon it by force of will. The soul can be approached only by reflection. Only through the mirror will the great changes ahead reveal themselves.

Your passage requires the ultimate dichotomy – to do without doing. For the soul is not found so much as it watches from the shadows, waiting for your moment of readiness to arrive. Only when the time is right will the door swing open. Only when you are ready will it step from those shadows and make itself known. Until then, be cognizant of the moment at hand, and focus on each step along the way. Set aside your need to monitor progress, or even to advance at all, for it will only make the going more difficult, and reinforce any misperception that this awakening comes solely as a result of the assertion of your will or desire.

While you make this spiritual journey of conscious choice, the opportunity for your illumined travel comes only by the grace of God. By your own power you do nothing. All happens only as an expression of the Will of God. Even your fervent intent to become whole is not the product of your conscious thought. It is generated by your soul, acting under the guidance of the divine. Only by the Divine Will can the needed changes occur so you can approach the door to the soul. Give yourself up in service, and invite God to work through you. Allow Him to fill your voice, and sing His song of love to the world.

A Puzzle Without Pieces

The journey to light is like assembling a puzzle for which you have neither a picture of what it should look like once completed, nor its pieces that are hidden as if objects in a scavenger hunt. The picture exists only in your mind until you have recovered them all. That image will be clouded so long as the mind distorts the certainty of your vision. Even then, it may remain obscured if even one piece is missing.

Not all that you uncover will be a piece to the puzzle. False pieces are scattered among the jewels that await your discovery. Only your soul knows what is of value on your journey. Test everything, for only through the right use of your intuition will you know which is which.

Follow only those that are true, lest you be led astray. Each new piece comes with instructions. Change this, do that, go here, then there, it may say. The direction you receive could lead to the next piece of the puzzle, or it may lead nowhere at all. The choice to follow is always yours. What will you do? Will you backtrack to where you strayed and resume your search? Will you walk a while further in hope that next clue will appear? Or will you simply give up your search, and remain where you are? Not at the beginning, and not at the end. But with an unfinished puzzle in hand.

Enjoy the puzzle. It holds the key to life. In fact, it is your life.

Cultivation

Introduction to Cultivation

To this point, we have touched upon the underlying reasons why man must make this journey within. However, we have dwelt little on the process that leads to awakening of the soul, other than to suggest that it begins inside.

King Arthur searched the land without success to find the Holy Grail, the cup of life. That is because it can never be found in the outer world. No matter where you look, it cannot be seen. No matter how far you search, it cannot be found. For the key to life can only be found in the inner world of the spirit. Though spirit is manifested in the outer world, it only leaves behind its imprint, and never the foot that made it.

Born to Roam

A man is born
to roam this land
in search far and wide
to discover
that which he has inside
and has known all along

We can only glimpse the nature of our soul if we first know ourselves. This is perhaps the most difficult part of the journey, for to know where we are going, we first must know where we start.

It requires that we see ourselves as we truly are, without the sweet façade our egos normally paint.

We look at ourselves all the time, yet so little do we see. Even when we look in the mirror we only see what we want, and turn a blind eye to the rest that appears before us. Sometimes we are startled when we fail to recognize the face that looks back at us. It is as if a stranger hides behind our eyes. These moments are invitations from our souls to venture beyond the shell to find what is hidden inside.

This is the journey we are about to undertake. It is a journey of transformation, for it requires us to practice the master's teaching, "Know thyself." But how do we do know ourselves? The mirror reflects only that which we choose to show the world. Those aspects we jealously guard from others are often just as hidden from us as well, and never see the light of day. We must zealously dig them out if we are to meet the soul that awaits us. Self-examination challenges us to look at ourselves critically, and if necessary burst the bubble of our self-deception to see that we are less than perfect. It frees us of the façade behind which we hide to see what we really are, so can we know where our transformation must begin.

The Mirror

I look in the mirror
And see
A deep, dark well,
And who
Is hiding at the bottom
But me

Our journey to the light only begins with this self-examination. Knowing helps us recognize what we are, not what we must become. We still lack any sense of what that is, much less how to get there. As we become more aware of our travel on this spiritual journey, our souls urge us to seek a clearer picture of what our "becoming" will bring, and undertake the effort necessary to bring conform ourselves to that image. It is in response to this call that we begin our inner transformation. However, even knowing what to do is not enough; we must walk the walk as well. This is through cultivation.

Just as the farmer cultivates the soil, preparing it to accept the seed in hope it will grow and nourish him in the days to come, so the spiritual warrior cultivates himself so that his spiritual seed will flourish. Cultivation prepares our inner soil, cutting the roots of the old ways, breaking their attachments to make room for the new seed to sprout and grow. It readies us to receive the light of love, and in turn reflect it to all within reach. Yet cultivation is not just limited to ways of the heart. Cultivation attends equally to the body, emotions, and mind so that no part of us is left behind. Each is carefully prepared to play its role in the process.

Cultivation not only softens the soil to receive the seed; it also casts out the impurities left by countless lifetimes spent blindly wandering in the wilderness. These impurities are more than unwanted characteristics. On an energetic level, action that conflicts with the spiritual laws agitates the vibrations of our auras, clouding them much like a river turns brown from the silt it stirs up below. Cultivation purifies the body's energy field, and prepares it to receive the tone of the soul.

If you are like most, your ground is hardened and not yet ready for planting. Some ideas you may reject wholeheartedly. Some may seem too hard to even attempt, for you have not prepared the soil where they can grow. Or you may try for a while, but old habits will soon push them aside.

Alas, this is the difficulty of the path. There is no single act that can prepare you to receive the seed of awakening. It encompasses a myriad of activities, many of which dull the imagination. Little of our work will appear to have anything do with traveling the spiritual path. Appearances, though, are as deceiving as the dream we live. Do not discount these ways simply because you do not fully comprehend their significance. Or because you have heard them countless times before. Handed down from generation to generation, they form the bedrock upon which the world's great religions are built. Here, though, we will delve beneath their foundations to see why and how to make them part of your life. Even if this new perspective conflicts with beliefs you now hold dear, will you not at least test them with your intuition, and allow it to guide you in their application?

Despair not if your ground is still hardened, or if you think you are unsuited to the ways presented here. The completion of your journey is as guaranteed as that of the most advanced along the path if you will but put forth the effort to prepare as is here and elsewhere written. Seek the spirit and you will find it. This is the way. Even so, you have made only a start.

Cultivation focuses attention upon aspects of your being that until now you may have taken for granted. As you do, you may begin to think they hold you back along your journey. Body, emotions, and mind combine to shape the experiences of your life. Too many fail to appreciate their importance and approach their journey as if certain aspects of our selves are enemies to be vanquished.

The body is the vehicle of our action in the tangible world. Its health allows us the opportunity to experience and interact with the world around us. Cultivation acts upon the energetic nature of that body to allow greater use of the energies that flow into it, and to heal the diseases that often hold it back.

Emotions often seem the bane of the *chela*[4], disturbing the equilibrium and complicating relationships. However, they bring a richness and quality to our experience than cannot be attained through physiological stimulus and mental response alone. Cultivation acknowledges their value, and acts to clip the peaks and valleys encountered along the way.

The mind is also an instrument for cultivation. Some try to squelch the activity of the mind, thinking that its activity is detrimental to one-pointed concentration in meditation as discussed below. Instead, it is a tool to be used and not cast aside. The untrained mind is like a wild stallion that does whatever and whenever it wants. Beautiful to behold, hard to stop, and even harder to tame, it resists all efforts to control it. Mind control is itself a misnomer. It suggests that the mind can be broken and made to

---

[4] *Chela* is the term given to a student on the spiritual path.

do our bidding. While we can break it, if we do, it will never serve the bidding of the awakened soul. Just as the broken stallion may become less than the lowliest plow horse, the mind is useless when forced to give up its ways. Broken, its will to live is gone. It retains its usefulness only if it changes of its own volition. To do that, it must first be convinced to abandon its anarchic world for one of peace and service of its master.

To enlist its help, you must afford it the same patience, love and respect we show the most revered who walk among us. With attentiveness you will grow aware of the thoughts that flit through your mind. With contemplation you will engage its abstract processes. And with loving attention you will encourage it to find the place of silence where the voice of the soul whispers its guidance.

At first you may not hear the voice when you call, and think it does not respond. Remain patient. It answers. It is just that you cannot yet discern it from the clutter of your mind. Even so, it will find a way to speak if you are ready to listen. It may come as a voice, or a thought slightly different than those you have known before. It may come as a feeling, or a sense of knowing that was not there before. Or it may come through the words of another, or an event of coincidence, that speaks to the very question you have asked or lesson at hand. No matter the medium or method of its response, it is up to you to hear it, and heed its call.

You must be willing to act as it guides you. For some, it may say that you are not ready, and to put down this book while its seed waits for another day to sprout. For others, it will suggest that these words have merit, and that you should read on and test them for yourself. No matter. Whatever its guidance, the soul knows what you need at your point of evolution.

When times seem harsh or the way uncertain, find the place of silence within. It will not be the end of your road, but it will be a source of your renewal. It will provide you with a place of solitude where you can rest, and gather strength for the tests ahead. It will bring you peace, and assure you that you are headed in the right direction.

Before you go on, rest a while. Seek the embrace of the silence. Sit quietly and bathe in its warmth. Know that it awaits you with open arms whenever you are in need, and that from its silence the voice will speak what you need to hear. When you are ready, join us. The road rises up ahead to greet you.

We will be waiting.

Free Will

Moment by moment, day after day, we live by our decisions. They separate us from the beasts that act on instinct alone. They give us power over the world. Our power of choice is called free will. It is the cornerstone of our cultivation.

Free will is an awesome power. Through it we craft our lives. We choose our actions and our reactions. We choose our thoughts, and our moments of no thought. We choose our desires, and also the moments we unleash our wills. We choose the values we live by, and the attitudes that paint the mask we show the world. We choose whether to live for personal gain, or to aspire to a higher cause. Even not choosing is an exercise of our free will – the choice to cast life to the fates, or to the whim of another's will. Choice after choice after choice fills our every waking moment.

Free will. The term itself is a misnomer. Although we have the power of choice to exercise our will, our choices are hardly free. Even the smallest decisions can have life-changing consequences. Through free will we shape our lives, and craft the circumstances that can allow our spirits to soar or shackle us with the heavy yoke of responsibility. Too often we crumble under the enormity of its weight.

Some even labor under the misguided belief that they have no choice and are just victims of others' actions. This misconception binds them to the past, and keeps them from moving into that place where the soul dwells. We are not victims, nor are we leaves helplessly bandied about by the winds of fate. Life is not thrust upon us. We participate every step of the way. The road of life forks many times; each time we choose which way we go.

Caught Between Worlds

Caught between worlds, so clearly I see
All that which I am and that which could be
Bound by chains forged from choices by me
Yet though in my hand I hold now the key
Unwilling am I to set myself free

This does not mean that we have control over the results of our decisions, or even the seemingly random events of our lives. Those are determined by a higher power, and written in the Divine Plan; they remain unknown until they unfold. Without sight to foretell the ending, the script we write is notably incomplete. The result is unsettling. On the one hand, we choose the fork that we will take on our walk through life. On the other, we cannot see where that path leads, and we find ourselves impotent to control the vagaries of what that path holds in store. Those choices lead us to new circumstances that seem beyond our control. Yet would they have happened if we had chosen another way? Our uncertainty breeds such a delicious discomfort, doesn't it?

The path of light requires a willingness to bear the weight of responsibility if we do not build the lives we want. There is no one else that can carry if for us, yet so often we assign blame to shift this responsibility onto others. This blame says they are the cause of our misery or misfortune.

Blame creates a victim mentality that we lack the power, authority, and responsibility for what happens in our lives. These thoughts are self-limiting, keeping us from tapping into God's abundance to create the results we crave. We have no hope to do this if cannot even acknowledge our role in the process. Blame abdicates our ability to choose, and denies us the rewards we crave.

Blame demonstrates we have not surrendered to the will of God. It shows we still bow in subservience to the rule of desire, thwarted at least momentarily from the result it seeks. What we don't know is that we will never get the peace that comes from living in the light until we accept whatever each roll of the dice brings. Know that while you alone have the power and duty to choose, only God determines the results. Choose, accept what comes, and then move on. The rest will take care of itself.

Finding Your Spiritual Compass

It is one thing to talk about exercising free will on our walk through life. It is quite another to do so, for we are given little instruction on how to do this. It would seem that we should just haphazardly choose, and wait to see what happens. Then if things don't work out, we should just pick up the pieces and move on. This is half the battle, for at least in this scenario we have regained power over our lives by avoiding the tendency to assign blame.

However, the inquiring mind will want to do more than just choose a door with no say in the outcome, for to do so is like selecting a fate by throwing darts at a board. It will quickly seize upon the real question at hand, which is, "How am I to make my life's choices in accord with that which God has planned for me?"

You are not left to fend for yourself in this perilous world. For though you may not have a clue where you are going or why, your soul does. It holds a map for your journey of life and the compass that points to your spiritual north. If you will listen, your soul will show you the way through the darkness that now surrounds you.

In the final instance, however, your test is not if you can hear it, but whether you will listen. Can you set aside the false promises of self-interest and desire to follow its lead? The serpent in the garden is always there to entice you. You will never find your way home if you succumb to its entreaties and stop to taste the fruits of the tree of desire.

What will you do?

Karma

The exercise of free will invokes the law of cause and effect. Desire is the cause; karma is the effect. Karma is the baggage of the soul. It is a limitation imposed by the totality of our existence from which we cannot escape, the boundary through which we cannot pass free of the weight of our experience.

In more common terms, karma is a pack we carry from life to life into which we place the stones of our desires. With each new desire we add it grows a little heavier, until we are so burdened by the desires of our past that we are unable to step lightly into the future.

When the exercise of choice is motivated by desire, it creates a debt that must be repaid. Sooner or later this karmic debt will come due. When that time will come is not up to us. It may come in this life, or in some life to come. But it will come.

Karma plays out in many ways, most of which are considered negative (though positive and negative have little meaning in terms of the growth of the soul). Accidents, misfortune, illness, and even death can result from its discharge to teach us the lessons of our errant ways.

Somewhere along the way we have to put down this weight of our desire before we can ascend to the light. Thankfully it is never too late to address our karmic burden, even when our backs are near breaking. The future is never etched in stone. It is constructed from the choices we make and the desires we manifest during our lives. Each moment is created from the choices of the ones before. Changing the foundation upon which those choices are based will change the resulting future as well.

The implications of this are enormous, and the spiritual warrior will do well to consider this wisely. The choices we make now affect not only our present, but also the future of this life and lives to come. Since free will gives us the power to choose our thoughts and desires, by careful choice we can also choose whether to create karma that we must sooner or later work off. The task before those who seek the light is to live so that each new moment is free of burdens generated by those that came before. The spiritual warrior grows ever more vigilant in the face of desire, knowing that each new fancy to which he succumbs burdens him with a debt he must someday pay. Thoughts and deeds are chosen carefully, for they lay the karmic foundation upon which the future is constructed. Desire is replaced by higher aspiration, which comes free of the weight.

Moreover, not only can we avoid creating karma to impact the future, we can also apply the law of cause and effect to reverse the karma of our past. When we walk the spiritual path, we begin to lay down some of the karma in our pack. Living free of desire while aspiring to serve the Will of God avoids creating new karma and transmutes existing karma into a force for good in our lives. It counteracts negative karma by constructing a "reservoir of grace" that will rain gifts upon our lives to come and raise us higher up the path of spiritual advancement. Only in this way can our pasts can be left behind, and we build the future to which we aspire.

Those who travel the spiritual path exercise their free will responsibly. They choose only thoughts and deeds that will bring them closer to unification. Through conscious exercise of each moment's choices, they free the future of the debt of the past and lay the groundwork for the awakening that beckons them.

To those who have not yet started upon the path, I implore you. You hold the key to your future. The choice is yours. What will you do with it? Will you suffer karma's wrath rather than give up your desires in service of a greater cause? Are you so addicted to your pleasures that you would risk them spilling out into your life and harming all that you hold dear? Or would you sacrifice your gratification to be free from the burden of your desires?

He who was without sin sacrificed his life incarnate to point the way for all to follow. He died to prove our addiction to suffering, and that we would bear any pain just to preserve our hope for pleasures ahead. If He would do that for the world, what sacrifice is too great for you to make for those you love, or the Plan you serve? Even if you think only of yourself, what price would you pay for a future life free from karma's weight?

This is the burden of your choice. You must bear it wisely, for the future rests in your hands. How will you choose?

Living in the Moment

Behind the senses, behind the mind, behind all that we know, there is one that lurks in the shadows. Watching. Waiting. Forever patient. Forever gathering information. It is the great observer. It is the watcher. It is the soul.

The watching soul sees all. It absorbs all the experience and sensation that this lifetime has to offer, even that which escapes the attention of the conscious mind and slips into the shadow realm of the subconscious. It gathers these experiences of a lifetime and assimilates them into our higher consciousness. Along the way, the desires and events are passed on to the universal mind to become part of the akashic record, leaving only life's sensations to take on our journey, along with knowledge and growth we acquire.

Our physical eyes see in the present, not the past or future. The soul, too, only sees in the moment. To the soul there is no past. There is no future. There is only the now, where all of life's sensations are gathered, experienced, and stored.

Life is now. This is where the attention should be focused, not on yesterday or tomorrow. Those are creations of a mind unable to let go of the past or live with no more than a glimpse of the future. The spirit dwells only in the now. It is only in the now where the spirit will reveal itself. It is only in the present that moments of understanding will come. These moments we call enlightenment.

Enlightenment is a guerrilla that strikes in stealth, and then departs just as quickly. Rather than wreaking havoc like the chaotic emotions, enlightenment leaves us in awe and compels us to search endlessly to recapture the moment lost. Later it may come again, bringing another moment of knowing, followed again by more searching. So we chase the light, hoping to banish the darkness from our lives. But we are doomed to fail if our eyes are fixed somewhere other than where we are.

The way to the moment is through the present, by living in the here and now. This requires our attention on each action and thought as it occurs. If we can focus our minds on when and where we are at a particular point in time, what went before becomes a shadow hiding from the light; what comes next is a dream better left undreamt.

The past and future are blindfolds, robbing us of sight of what occurs around us. While the rest of creation experiences the present, too often we are wrapped in the cocoon of our thoughts, unable to see. If we live in the past, or with our eyes locked on the future, we deny ourselves the chance to savor the splendor that surrounds us. What happened before is of no consequence, and dwelling upon yesterday or tomorrow detracts from experiencing today.

What once was, is now gone. Whatever will be, will be. But the now is always the now. There is no other time but now.

Life's Mountain

Life's mountain I climb
With back bent by memories
Stored like precious coins
In the pack of my life
Carried as gleaming reminders
Of what once was and will never again be
Their weight slows my ascent
Unable am I to discard them
And be on my way to the world that I seek

Past and future are the creations of the mind, distracting us from the events of the now. The mind remembers what was, and considers what might be. But the watcher is not distracted. It knows where all occurs. It exists here, and attends to the now.

The mind, though, is often anywhere but here and now. Unable to remain in the present, it wanders in its reverie; here and there, yesterday and tomorrow merge in an indistinguishable fog. No one is at the helm as the mind drifts in and out of life on autopilot.

The soul does not share its journey, and the gulf between them widens. Though forever linked, the rift is great. We truly seem alone.

When our attention is focused elsewhere in place or time, we are unable to work in harmony with the soul. We are left to our own devices, and to fend for ourselves. Without the soul's guidance, we are exposed to the world, bereft of shelter and stripped of our compass. We are truly lost and waiting to be saved.

To get to the moment is simultaneously easy and extraordinarily difficult. We only need to totally focus on whatever is at hand. Such concentration is tremendously liberating. It frees the mind from the garbage of the past or future, and silences much of the senseless chatter that clutters the mind. By redirecting attention to the circumstances of the present, our thoughts vanish into nothingness. It allows the observer inside to watch, without the mind's distracting comment, while we gather the experiences of life.

However, the attention is obstructed when we are burdened by desire. Desire whispers in our ear us to look beyond this moment to paint a picture of what it wants the future to bring. It triggers thoughts of something other than the now. Living in the moment allows the mind to let go of desire, for it cannot simultaneously focus on the present as well as the future where that desire is manifested.

Through attention to the moment, all other principles of cultivation become possible. Without it, we continue our walk of sleep, denied the chance to awaken from this dream. Either we make the most of it, or lose it forever.

If a moment lacks sufficient attention, we cannot relive it. Moreover, we cannot dwell on it or mourn its passing, for that chains us to the past. We can only return to the present.

Attention frees us to venture beyond the walls of our thought to take in whatever comes. It allows us to greet life and experience it as it occurs. Attention recognizes that life is only experience. Some we like. Others we don't. But they all are of value in our spiritual growth and service of humanity. Attention on the moment keeps us from trying to filter out the bad and skim off the good. It says that all who share our lives are important, and that together we will explore the great unknown that stretches out before us. It says that every moment, every breath, is important to us.

As well it should be. Life is a feast. Every moment brings another succulent morsel to savor. Every moment is special. Not even the most common and mundane of life's events are "boring" if we give them sufficient attention. Attention builds our awareness, and through it we develop appreciation for the wonders around us. It helps us re-shape our attitude with appreciation in place of expectation.

Attentiveness frees us from the chains of what went before, and the enticement of what may never be. It brings life into our field of awareness so we can cultivate an appreciation for all of creation. It allows us to experience the exhilaration of being alive. It brings the world to life.

Imagine the wonders that have passed to which you were blind! What things were staring you in the face, but you refused to take them in? How can you let another moment go by with soaking in all that it has to offer?

Life's Bucket

Drop after drop time leaks from life's bucket
Wasting away this precious gift we share
Day 'pon day filled chasing hollow treasures
Minds closed to thoughts of purpose for our stay
Aghast, one day we find it nearly empty
No trace or trail of moments left behind
Panicked hands cling tightly to the bucket
To savor now its few remaining drops
And leave us to cry,
"Why did we squander our time in the sun?"

Only if you concentrate your attention in the moment can you see every tree. Or greet the sunshine. Or hear the birds sing. Or feel the wind on your face, and the earth under your feet.

The greatest gift you can give yourself is to place your attention in the moment. Taste each sensation. Touch every heart! Greet every moment with equal passion. Do not let even one minute come and go without breaking the surface of your awareness. Focus your attention and savor life; make it yours. This is where the spirit lives. This is where you must be, for it is with full attention that the spiritual warrior meets the moment. Focusing attention in the moment brings awareness of the world around us where our life's experiences play out. It results from an appreciation for life, and how special the gift of each moment truly is. Incarnation is wasted if you are elsewhere or when. This moment will never again be repeated for all eternity. If you blink, it is gone forever. You get no chance to do it again.

All it takes is the intention to experience the moment. And appreciate it when it arrives.

Thanks

Thank you
For the gift of this breath
And moment
Never to be repeated
In all
Eternity

Love

What can be said about love that has not been said so many times before, in so many different ways? Words cannot hope to adequately describe this most elusive and sought after force, but there is no need to try. For if those who read these passages do not yet know what love is, there is naught I can say that will give them that knowledge. Here we are concerned only with the application of love, not the semantics that the mind can play trying to put into worldly terms that which is not of this world.

Jesus implored us to love our neighbors as we love ourselves. But do we love ourselves? Too often we turn a blind eye to the one that dwells inside. We pretend to ignore it in fear that we may lose what little appearance of control we have over life. If it is so bad that we must hide it away, how can we love ourselves? If we cannot love ourselves, then should we love anyone else more? Can we?

Self-image is a fragile concept. If we look too closely, it may break, and we may not like what we find. We see ourselves as peaceful beings, yet at the first sign of provocation respond by vicious counterattack. We think of ourselves as caring, but turn our backs on those without sufficient food, clothing, or shelter. We even believe we are kind-hearted (some may even say philanthropic or charitable), yet we fight to grab a bigger piece of the pie so that someone else won't get it. Is this how we love ourselves? We deceive ourselves through false images of us, as well as how we treat others. How sad.

Love's first precept is to be true to yourself. You cannot hope to love others unless you first know how to love yourself. You cannot know how to love yourself until you wash away all of the false conceptions you hold and false promises you make. If desire blinds you to your true needs, then how can you know what to pursue? To be true to yourself is not to be true to your desires – it demands truth to the one at the center – your soul.

If there is any common feeling inside the human vehicle, it is the craving to be loved. Too many go through life in a state of denial, denying love to themselves and to others as well. By doing so, they subtly say to others they don't have any love to give them.

What is Love?

What is this thing called Love of which you spoke
Over which wars are fought and hearts are broke?
What is its pull upon the soul of man
To trade joy for grief and then back again?
What is this thing called Love I must you ask
That harbers ill when mirrored not to bask
In reflected glow giv'n without return?
So bittersweet this nectar of life's urn
Why this mask
We live to wear, then once had we spurn?

The problem is most look for love in all the wrong places. We think love comes from others, so we live life thinking that others should do to us what we want them to. This is not the way of love. Love demands we treat others the way we want to be treated, no matter how they treat us.

We look for love everywhere but where we are. Love is not found in others. Love is not found in things. Love is not found in the circumstances of life. Love is found only within us. There it waits until we prepare ourselves to receive it. Until we find the love that is ours, we have nothing to share with others. We have nothing with which to apply the words, "Love thy neighbor." We have not found the love of God that flows through our soul and wells up from its spring within us.

Yet, this love is easy to find. It is there for the taking. It requires nothing from us, or from those with whom we choose to share it, other than unleashing it to work its magic in the world. Still, even when we find it, we don't put it to work. Instead of inviting it into our lives, we hoard it, thinking we'll save it for those few people we really want to grace with its gift. Little do we know that we are the ones in need, and that by locking it away, we deny ourselves its precious touch.

Love is not discriminating. It knows not whether we are "good" or "bad." It knows not whether another is friend or foe, family or stranger. It knows not whether we "like" or "dislike" another. It only knows love. This love, the love of the spirit, is unconditional. It needs no reciprocity. It exists solely to be set free.

Love is our Creator's gift to us. It gives us that which is in him, together with all the powers of the worlds that wait beyond this one. It is the force with which he created our universe. Its magnificence cannot be put into words. It is pure feeling. It is the essence of the soul, which manifests itself in this world through love. Through love, it cracks opens the door between planes, and once through, kicks it in.

The Key

Love is the key
To free our hearts
Its light shows us the way
To use it

We must give it away
To bask in its glow
And unlock the door
To our souls

Love opens the heart to allow the light of the spirit to pour out and bathe all in its glow. What's more, love freed unlocks the hearts of those it touches, hastening their awakening as well. All who are touched by love are transformed. But none can be touched by our love until we are. We cannot love our neighbors until we first love ourselves. Not love of self, but the love of the spirit for its child, its creation in this world.

Even if we decide we are ready to open ourselves to love, this may not be enough. Like the summer rains whose flash floods race out of control over the hardened ground, love often washes over us before we are ready, and spills upon our unprepared ground. It is wasted if we are not ready for it.

The heart is a well filled by an endless spring of love. It bubbles from within, then spills out so its magic can spread. If the well is cracked or riddled with holes, it will never fill. Love will leak out before it can be used. If the well is poisoned with hate or envy or desire, there is sparse room for the love to enter, and the little that does may cause illness or worse. Our task is to purify the well of our heart, and prepare it to receive and hold the love that awaits us.

We do this through our practice of cultivation. It readies our container, sealing its holes and removing the impurities that poison the well. Cultivation prepares our inner ground to receive love, and teaches us what to do with it once it is ours. But without the nourishment of love, the seed of awakening will die, just as the farmer's seed will die if casually tossed on fallow soil and denied the life-giving rains from above.

As we inspect the walls of our heart, our eyes focus on the cracks and holes. The light is harsh; our blemishes are many. "My heart can never be repaired to hold the love," we exclaim to ourselves. Many give up, thinking themselves unworthy, and that the task is too great. These blemishes, which some call sins, are obstacles we have built between our hearts and the love that is already ours. They block the entrance through which love flows and deny us its healing touch.

The impurities of our lives must be removed, one by one, until love flows freely into every corner of our lives. But the work ahead is not easy. Some of the obstacles will dissolve quickly. Others may take repeated effort. Many more may remain tucked away in dark corners from where they shoot out their invisible tentacles to barricade the door to our hearts, shutting out the love that seeks to enter. Their chains are forged from the hardness of our hearts. We can deny them. We can ignore them. But we cannot break them without love. Somehow we must first find the love that awaits us, and turn it upon ourselves to heal our injuries and open the way for more to follow.

If we are truly willing to submit ourselves to love's mercy, nothing can withstand its might. Love is like the life-giving water of the physical world. It nourishes our souls and breathes life where none appeared before. An insidious, irresistible force, love seeps into every crevice. It soaks into every pore. It washes away the resistance of immovable objects. Just as the water cuts great canyons into the face of the earth, love works its way through the cracks of even the hardest of hearts. Slowly, softly, but ever so insistently, it bubbles up inside until the heart awakens from its slumber. Once healed and its blemishes closed, the heart becomes as soft and supple as the fresh-bloomed rose. Finally, it opens and spills out into the world, in search of a new heart to touch.

Even then, vigilance is needed to insure that once love's rose opens, its petals will close no more to stem its flow into the world. Love hoarded is love denied. Locked away, it withdraws back into the soul. Without it to nourish our hearts, we will shrivel and die inside.

There is no reason to hide love away. It can never be diminished; its source is inexhaustible. In wave after wave, it wells up from the spiritual plane to flow through our soul to our hearts and into the world. As long as the door to our hearts remains open, the love we set free is continually replenished.

Learn the ways of love, and apply them in all aspects of life. Let love fill your heart and guide your way each moment of every day. Only in this way can you awaken to your soul.

The Lieutenants of Love

The ways of love are applied through compassion, non-judgment, and forgiveness. These are the three lieutenants of love, waging love's war against the forces of darkness. They lead its soldiers in the trenches, and mobilize the missionaries that spread the light of love throughout the world. These three teach us how to put love's power to work in the world. Through them we overcome all that stands in the way of the soul's entry into the world.

Compassion

Compassion is love in action. It is through our compassion that we put love to work. Compassion directs our love to others. It allows us to feel their pain, and compels us to try to relieve it. It enables us to ease the impact of their circumstances in life.

Compassion recognizes that other souls may not be as far along the path of awakening as we are, and bids us to shine a light upon their way. It knows that the trials others face may be more than they can deal with, and extends a hand to pull them through the test. It allows love to work through us as an instrument of its expression.

Too often, though, we fail to heed its call. When we see a starving child, how do we respond? Do we turn our backs and ignore it? If so, then we lock our love away and hoard it for a rainy day that may never come.

Compassion compels us to act. If we see a hungry child, we feed it. If the child is hurt, we tend its wounds. If it is crying, we dry its tears and try to mend its heart. If it is uncertain which way to turn, we lead it to the path and hold its hand until it can walk alone. If it suffers, we remove the source of its pain.

Hide the Children

Swollen bellies
Hollow eyes
Ragged clothing
Hungry cries

Furtive glances
Quickened strides
Deafened ears
Blinded eyes

Hide the children
Tell us lies
Lest their pain
Our hearts divide

Our hearts naturally open to children, for they wear the innocence of youth. The real test is to open them as widely to the rest of society – to the sick, the poor, the downtrodden, or those who simply are not as fortunate as we. They bear the scars of society's wars, relegated to the forgotten zone, shunned in hope their pain will not become our own. They, too, need our hand. They, too, must be extended the touch of our hearts to ease their pain. Though suffering is carried by every man, it is a burden that none deserve to carry. Love motivates us to ease it when we can.

We share the light that burns within us. Though separated through incarnation, we are each a part of the whole, the source, our God. Our brothers and sisters in pain are as much a part of God, and He of them, as are we.

We engage in charity when we direct love compassionately toward our neighbors in need whose life's circumstances are less fortunate than our own. It is the ultimate expression of love in the world, putting it to work and returning it to its source. Charity is an act of compassion. It is "love directed first toward God, but also toward oneself and one's neighbors as objects of God's love."[5]

Charity in modern society is less an expression of compassion than a disguised search for self-reward. Too often our charity is given so we in turn will receive benefit. Giving our money or clothing or food so that we can get a good feeling about ourselves. Giving our property so that we will be taxed less. Giving our time in hope that the exposure will generate revenue down the road. Where have we gone wrong?

True charity is given without expectation of return of any kind. It expresses compassion given out of love and nothing else, and is best performed on a soul-to-soul basis. This personal contact is critical, for it helps to awaken the souls of both giver and recipient. Charity freely and directly given builds a conduit through which souls can share pain, and receive another's love to release it. Charity through compassionate action reunites souls separated in their journey through this life. Charity through others denies everyone this opportunity.

Compassion does not always flow freely from our hearts. It must be cultivated, as much as the love in our hearts. It allows us to serve through love. If we do so with the needs of others truly in mind, and not to advance our own, we may later revel in the magnificence of the awakening. If good deeds are performed solely with the intent to prepare us for that event, it will never arrive. This is the great dichotomy. We seek without seeking; we seek by serving.

Non-Judgment

Judgment is a wall that emphasizes our separateness from the others who inhabit this world. It damns the flow of love into the world. It is overcome by even greater love, for love allows us to overlook

---

[5] *The American Heritage Dictionary of the English Language, Fourth Edition,* Houghton Mifflin Company (2000).

those faults and focus on the spirit inside. Love does not turn a blind eye. It sees the faults, and accepts them anyway. Even where the fault does harm, love allows us to let go of responsive emotions that interfere with our awakening.

Our preoccupation with these faults blinds us to our true nature, allowing us to see only that which does not meet up to our standards. We are so absorbed within the shells that we have created for ourselves that we are loathe to grant another even the smallest of leeway in their transgressions. Our minds generate a silent dialogue critiquing most that we see, refusing to accept less than perfection. Worse, we share those thoughts, making critical remarks that cut to the quick without concern. Judgment quickly becomes a tool of aggression, a means of asserting our will.

Judgment sanctifies the mind's perception that we are omnipotent beings at the center of our universe. It reinforces the walls of distinction that separate us from the rest of the world. Judgment wields the sword of our retribution when others are less than what we want them to be, because we expect them to be other than what they are. They do not match the mental picture we have created for them, and when we compare them to our image, we become outraged. How dare they blaspheme against our rule? When they fail to stand up to our scrutiny, we assert our dominance by punishing them through our judgment. We are lawmaker, prosecutor, judge and jury. We are gods.

The Gods

As if gods
We assert our wills
Over the domain of our desires
Making war
On the infidels
Who blaspheme
To contest our rule

Judgment wraps itself in a cloak of righteousness that its desire of the moment is the way things must be. With the air of an infallible ruler, we wield our judgment so often that little of the world is seen without its blemishes. Not much is the way we want it to be, so we condemn all that does not meet our standards. We grow negative and bitter that it does not meet our image. We have planted and sown the seeds of our own unhappiness.

Often judgment goes beyond mere observation and condemnation, and triggers some retaliatory action against the perceived offender. Between individuals, conflicts of wills result, often with some statement or action exerted to let the other know of their transgression. They may fight back, justifying their actions to their own minds and hoping to convince ours, escalating the wrath of judgment even further. Judgment then begets conflict, and the cycle continues.

Our judgment is not reserved for the transgressions of others. We direct its greatest fury at the one in the mirror, for we are never what we want ourselves to be. Self-judgment brings the burden of guilt. It weighs us down and distracts attention from the moment to the past. It reminds us we are not what we think we should be, building a barrier to self-acceptance and further impeding the flow of love into our hearts. Judgment stops us from loving ourselves. It is the ultimate punishment.

We must not judge others or us if we want to move beyond this plane. None now on earth are perfect. We each have weaknesses to conquer. Who should cast the first stone? No one is superior to another; we are all the same. Moreover, we have incarnated to live the respective lives we live, and gather the growth that they bring. We helped to plot those lives before we were born to attain the lessons they were meant to give, while at the same time fulfilling our roles in the Divine Plan. We cannot now judge it wrong because we lack the vision to see how actions fit that Plan. Yet that is what we do. When we judge, we imply that we are more knowledgeable than our Creator, and that the plan for our lives is insignificant. How can this be? If we accept that there is a Divine Plan, and that the lives we live express that Plan, then all things are as they should be. Judgment stands in the way of that realization, and denies us peace on earth.

Jesus also taught us not to judge others so that we won't be judged. Our judgment slams shut the door to the spiritual world. When we turn our back on the Plan, it turns its back on us. When that happens, we are judged unworthy of the responsibilities we were born to assume. We are judged sons and daughters of desire and not of the spirit. We are judged to live without the force of love in our lives. On the path, there is no room for judgment. Attention must be firmly fixed upon the light, and through that search, our service of the Plan. Let us judge not, so that we will not be judged for our failure to complete that search, nor be denied the tools needed for our journey.

Forgiveness

Forgiveness walks hand in hand with judgment. Through forgiveness we tell the world that bygones will be bygones – the past is past and so it shall remain. It closes the door to the past, and brings the attention to the moment. It is a clear message to others that what they have done will not be held against them. It is acceptance, notwithstanding the transgression. Forgiveness is the ultimate act of love.

Too often, not only do we judge, but we also harbor grudges. Without forgiveness, we wield the sword of retribution as a continuing reminder that an act breached the sanctity of our desire. This retribution punishes both the transgressor and us as well, for it refuses to allow the moment to move smoothly into the past, and instead carries it with us into the future. It forces the mind to live in the past, and to extend its desires into the future. As judgment after judgment builds up, these acts of non-forgiveness chain us to what once was and deny us the present that is ours.

Forgiveness is not some gift we graciously bestow on someone who transgresses against our desires. Forgiveness is a gift we give ourselves, recognizing first that non-forgiveness denies us the moment, and second, that we all share a common bond. The other person is not different from us. He is a part of us. By forgiving him, we forgive ourselves as well.

Forgiveness must be in our hearts at all times if we hope to see and gain admission into the next plane. God lives within each of us, but can only be seen in the moment. Forgiveness allows us to stay in this moment, so that our eyes may see that which has been ours all along. We put the past to bed when we forgive, and return our attention to the moment. The soul can only live in the now. Dwelling on the past directs our energy other than to the moment, and prevents the soul from awakening.

Man's imperfection imposes faults on us all; love allows us to overlook them. It acts through forgiveness to focus on the spirit inside. Overlooking faults does not mean to turn a blind eye. Instead, love compels us to see the faults, and accept them anyway. Forgiveness helps us let go of the anger and other emotions that keep us from awakening.

Forgiveness is the supreme test of love, for it tests our ability to see imperfections yet have the willingness to excuse them. It puts us in control of the lessons we take from this life. We are never victims when we forgive; we accept life's lessons for what they are. Life is a mirror, reflecting back the lessons we are here to acquire. Those lessons begin with us, for we must forgive ourselves of our own shortcomings as well. Love can never fill our hearts until we recognize that inside we are already perfect, and accept the way we are.

Forgiveness is not some gift we charitably bestow upon someone who is somehow less than we are. Others are part of us, as we are of them. By forgiving them, we forgive ourselves. Through forgiveness we bring love into our own lives, and reflect our progress along the path of awakening. It is the ultimate act of love to leave the past behind and move on. When we live with forgiveness we accept others as they are. It says, "I know you are different from me, but that is the way it should be. We are together on this walk through life as equals, not one better than another. Come walk awhile with me."

Forgiveness is the supreme test of love. Forgiveness is love's way of encountering transgressions, and then excusing the offense. It puts us in control of the lessons we take from this life. When forgiveness is our way of expressing love, we cannot see ourselves as victims of the actions of others. Their deeds simply were, and are no more.

As the Lord's Prayer said, "… Forgive us our trespasses, as we forgive those who trespass against us …." If we do not forgive theirs, who will forgive ours?

Do No Harm

Do no harm. This principle of cultivation addresses acts of the physical body, however motivated. It requires we cultivate harmlessness. It demands we live under the rule of love in all things and all ways.

Its implications are many. Take no life. Do not hurt another with your thoughts or deeds. Restrain your words, lest you wield them as knives that cut to the quick. Temper your actions as well as your reactions. When attacked, turn the other cheek; do not retaliate.

We are already estranged from our souls. Every act of harm we do puts another brick in the wall that separates us from the spirit, moving it a little farther out of reach. Harm is insidious; it seeps its way into all aspects of life. It hardens our hearts and perpetuates a cycle of destruction that poisons the world.

Harm is not just inflicted upon others; we bring its wrath down upon us as well. We think ourselves inept when results do not meet our expectations. We judge ourselves weak when we succumb to our desires. And we routinely live without sufficient attention to the moment, and then wonder where our lives have gone. What can another do that is worse than that we do to ourselves?

But still we compete to see who can inflict the greatest harm. Nations defend their man-made borders by threatening mutual destruction. Women are raped in orgies of power and unleashed desire. And men routinely assault and kill their fellow men, justified by whatever strikes their fancy of the moment.

Harm comes in more insidious ways as well. The means of production and channels of capital deprive many of needed food to the point of starvation. Natural resources are depleted to build more "things" we can do without. We pollute the water we drink and the air we breathe, all in the name of progress. At what cost? How can we think we've progressed, if we haven't learned even the simplest lessons of love given so many centuries ago?

These dense physical bodies promote a mistaken belief that we are all separate. This perception of uniqueness misleads us into thinking that what we do affects only those against whom it is directed. We forget, or maybe do not understand, that we all share a common bond with our Creator. God truly does reside within us; His energy is our life force. Doing harm attacks the part of us that we all share. It is an attack on us as well.

To do no harm cultivates a respect for life. All of creation, no matter how small or seemingly insignificant, plays a role in the Divine Plan. Each has a soul; our assault devalues the spirit behind it. Each shares a connection with the others. Harm to one harms all; it harms us as well.

Callous disregard for life denigrates the value of all beings in this dimension and beyond. It implies arrogance that we are supreme above all, and that our will and desires are paramount to the Divine Plan of creation. We walk in darkness. Let us not stub our toe before the light shines upon us.

Harmlessness extends far beyond our physical acts, for much of the harm we inflict is not upon the bodies of others. We assault their minds instead through our speech. Some think it civilized to replace physical harm with mental harm. Yet the wounds inflicted by our words strike even more deeply than all but the most vicious physical attack, and last even longer.

Thoughtless comments about appearance or character can alter a self-image for life. Tone of voice can precipitate conflict. Sarcasm may imply superiority, provoking a response to prove otherwise. We think we are strong, yet we shrink before the poisoned barbs of others, all the while absorbing their poison deep within our psyche. And doing it to them as well.

Sometimes the most destructive attacks are not the outright vicious assaults of verbal warfare. Criticism cuts to the bone, no matter how well meant. Even helpful suggestions are taken as an attack more often than not. Comments about physical stature or weight or intelligence or any other characteristic can build deeply seated neuroses, perhaps hidden from the world but nevertheless eating away at the innards of the recipient. Witness how deeply we're cut and quickly we defend when subjected to even the smallest criticism, no matter how well meant. Is it reasonable to expect even stronger words to pass without impact? Is this how we spread our love to the world?

Many also think it is alright to unleash their verbal assault on those whom we profess to love. The stresses of the day wear us down. Without the protective barriers reserved for the rest of the world, our venom spews forth. Harsh words, criticism, loud voices, personal attacks and counterattacks are all common fodder among those who share the bond of "love." Blinded to the truth, we unleash our verbal sword under the guise of justification. "They know I really love them." Even when a mistake is acknowledged, it is often sloughed off with a simple, "They know I didn't mean it." Meanwhile, this person we love is left to pick up the pieces of a broken heart left bleeding from the assault. Even good-natured suggestions are too often thinly disguised remarks that suggest, "I don't love you the way you are, so change." Is it any wonder that so many families carry so much baggage with them? Is it any wonder that baggage is then spread throughout the world?

If you choose the way of the spiritual warrior, you are cautioned to judiciously watch every sound you uttter, for the word has power. It is the source of creation, as well as destruction. Use it to build up the world, not tear it down. Be on guard not to use the word to inflict harm in any form. Do not allow your word to become the servant of the dark side. Take care that not even the slightest attack slips from your lips, lest it set back all the work that you do on other fronts. And watch even the tone of your voice, and the manner of your response, lest it convey anything other than your love. For as John said, "In the beginning was the Word."

Harmlessness in action is the Golden Rule applied. We do not want to suffer harm; how can we justify inflicting it upon others? They, too, need to be secure in their persons and minds. Why are we not willing to extend others the courtesy we expect for ourselves?

Whatever you do, wherever you go, do no harm. Show your love to the world.

Be Truthful

Let truth guide your life. Practice always telling the truth. Be honest with others and yourself.

Truth is an absolute. Something is either true, or it is not. Or so it would seem. For in some instances, truth is a matter of perception. What appears so from one view may not appear that way from another.

Does this make truth relative? Not necessarily. But it does impose on us a duty to evaluate facts from all sides, in order that we may ascertain what is in fact true. Sometimes multiple looks will render that impossible, for different perspectives may lead to differing views of events. At other times, it will lead to a new, unexpected conclusion, based upon the interaction of the views. Jumping to conclusions without considering alternative views does no justice to the truth.

Truth, then, gives the appearance that it is a matter for interpretation. As the mind must interpret the sensory data, so must it interpret facts to ascertain the truth. Like a jury sworn to impartially hear and decide the facts before the bar, the mind's ability to interpret, and often interpolate, is based upon its ability to perceive the different views without imposing the filter of its own will and desires. Bias distorts perception. Therefore to know the truth requires that we both know and understand our own biases, and have the ability to distance ourselves from them in order to arrive at a less colored version of the truth. The term "version of the truth" is used because we may never see or accurately interpret all facts relevant to such a determination, notwithstanding the absence of bias. Similarly, even where bias exists, an accurate perception of the "truth" remains possible (though less reliably so).

Yet, deep down, below the different perceptions, truth is an absolute. There is only one. If you are to know it, you must find it, and wear it around as a shield. Though it may at first hurt or be heavy, the truth will ultimately empower you to transcend the karma-manas (thought-desires) of the material world. Truth is the foundation for awakening, and upon its bedrock all cultivation must be laid. Evaluate all the possibilities. Look behind the actions to the desires, and behind the desires to the objects of pleasure that trigger them. Behind them all lies the truth. Find it.

Truth?

What is truth
And what is not
Is not for us to know
But just to seek
And catch a glimpse
While trapped
By the darkness
That surrounds our minds

Furthermore, no matter the semantics and possibilities for differing "truths," telling the truth foregoes the possibility of stating something that we know is not so. Purposely telling a falsehood compromises our own integrity while committing a wrong against others to whom it is spread. It is a poison that infiltrates our minds, putting our desire for a particular outcome ahead of our own integrity. Purification of the bodies demands it be free of such impurities. Therefore the telling of untruths is to be avoided by those on the path.

Untruthfulness reflects a desire to preserve the mind's self-interest. Desire is a flower to be ripped out of the heart;[6] falsehood is the spawn of that flower, spreading its unwanted seed throughout

---

[6] Collins, *Light on the Path, supra.*

the core of our being. To avoid further growth, we must cast aside its seed and never allow it to fall upon the inner soil we tend.

Do not even permit yourself to tell "white lies" on small, insignificant matters. Or say untruths to avoid causing discomfort or harm. Lies are lies, no matter the motivation. Intent cannot reshape the lie to make it acceptable. We who are locked in this world are in no position to decide what is harm and what is not, much less whether the truth or the perpetuated lie does the greater harm. What circumstance of the outer world is of greater importance than the needs of the soul within? The outer world is ever changing to our needs and perceptions. Unless your soul clearly guides you otherwise, the better course is to rely on the truth. Once a lie is unleashed, the harm is done and the well poisoned once again.

Consider this well. Through all the world's religions is found one version or another of the commandment, "Thou shall not lie." Yet men live with falsehood as a way of life. Why do men choose to live in direct violation of such a simple yet powerful rule of living? Why do men choose to violate any of the rules or commandments that they profess to accept? They do so because they determine it in their interest to do so. Desire to protect and promote self-interest (or in some cases the interests of others) is the paramount concern, even above the requirements of their own spiritual belief system.

Why is this? Is desire so powerful or important as to overcome even the most deeply held convictions? Is it simple expediency, taking the "easy" way out? Or is it that we just do not accept the supremacy of the command or its source? Or could it be that we do not truly believe there is an existence beyond this life that may in some manner be affected by our untruths now, so we act with only the desires of the moment in mind? After all, a lie is such a little thing.

In a word, yes. It is all of these. Reasoning is so easy. The mind is good at it. But what it is best at is the great delusion, convincing even itself that one excuse or another is sufficient reason to justify a wrongful act, because it does not know otherwise for certain.

The awakened mind will know what to do. It will pursue the

path of greatest service of the Plan, and growth of the soul This cannot occur so long as we continue to poison our bodies with falsehood. If aspiration and the desire to awaken are greater than the desire to protect our mind's perception of its self-interest, then we will choose the truth. If not, then truth will be pushed aside whenever the conflict becomes too great.

Again, you have come to a fork in the road. Which way will you travel?

Do Not Steal

Do not take that which is not yours. Control your physical actions notwithstanding a conflicting desire or mental inclination. Do not to succumb to the temptation to take from others the objects of your mind's desire. This requires the exercise of forbearance until the cause of craving is removed.

This commandment combats a powerful belief held by so many in the paramount importance of the outer world. What they crave to possess and take for themselves in the outer is more important than the dweller that calls from within. The traveler on the path of light knows this isn't so. It is the inner that rules, and nothing in the outer world is of greater importance than the light he seeks to free.

So many take what is not offered. So often we do it we don't even realize it occurs, and justify it as a matter of right. Either something is ours to do with as we please, or it is not. If it is not ours, then is it given us as a gift? If it is neither a gift, nor ours, how can we receive it with grace and appreciation? How can it express the love that emanates from our souls? How can it move us closer to the light?

We know the answer. It can't. Still, the insidious temptation of desire is often overwhelming. Lust blinds us to the reality that all abundance is ours if we will but open ourselves to that which our Father has provided.

As a result, this knowledge will make little difference until the awakened soul grabs so great a hold that we can do nothing but obey. Until then, our mission is to face the chasm between our knowing and actions, and accept out failures without condemnation or judgment. All we can do is bless our humaness, and commit to try again when the next test comes.

Besides, we can always rewrite the rules of life, and even use the great teachings of awakening to insure our fancies are well met.

What's Mine?

What's yours is yours, and mine is mine
Or so we're often told
Yet what you have is what I want
I'll get it if I'm bold.

If All we have belongs to God
Who lives inside of me
Then what you're holding is a gift
Received in trust for Me.

So now perhaps you see my plight
Though I may seem abrupt
Life's bounty that you hold so close
Is MINE, so give it up!

Losing Desire

We have touched on the impediments created by desire for those on the path of awakening. Desire attaches thoughts to a future that may never come. It judges others as if they were children of a lesser god. It triggers the emotions, and undermines our relationships. It follows us into this world, and chains us to it. Desire paints the dream that clouds our eyes.

Desire to be born brings us into this world. It creates the lives we live. And our desire to live keeps us here. The spiritual warrior would do well to recognize the connection between desire and existence in the three worlds. Desire barricades the bridge separating the worlds. The implications of its removal are of great significance to those seeking the light.

"Desire is attachment to objects of pleasure."[7] Whether those objects are things, places, or people, these objects exist only within the dream. Within it they are real, but from the perspective of our true existence in the spiritual world, it is a fog that covers our eyes. These objects arouse the sensation of pleasure, so the mind creates desire to try to hold onto this pleasure to keep it around a little while longer. We are so enamored with our perception of these objects in the fog, and the emotional reactions they generate, that we form attachments to them. These attachments must be broken if we hope to ever move beyond the dream.

---

[7] *The Light of the Soul, its Science and Effects: The Yoga Sutras of Patanjali with Commentary*, Alice Bailey and Djwhal Khul, Lucis Publishing Company (1998).

> *Seek in the heart the source of evil and expunge it. It lives fruitfully in the heart of the devoted disciple as well as in the heart of the man of desire. Only the strong can kill it out. The weak must wait for its growth, its fruition, its death. And it is a plant that lives and increases throughout the ages. It flowers when the man has accumulated unto himself innumerable existences. He who will enter upon the path of power must tear this thing out of his heart. And then the heart will bleed, and the whole life of man seem to be utterly dissolved. This ordeal must be endured; it may come at the first step of the perilous ladder which leads to the path of life: it may not come until the last. But, O disciple, remember that it has to be endured: and fasten the energies of your soul upon the task* [8]

Just the thought of severing desire's hold raises objection in all but the most advanced along the path. "Oh, no!" they cry. "We can't live without desire. Life would have no meaning." However, this concept is easily comprehended once past the emotional barrier. After all, it is commonly accepted that the will to live is an important element to preserve life for those whose bodies suffer illness or frailty. Lose it and death is imminent. Desire is our tether to this world.

The term "objects of pleasure" does not refer only to tangible experiences of the physical body. In fact, perhaps our greatest attachment is to thought itself. Whether memories of pleasures past, or images of pleasures hoping to come, the mind builds its desires upon the foundation of thought. In a sense, desire is the glue that holds the mind-stuff, the *chitta*, together. Without desire, the attention would not attach to the thoughts and they would soon be gone. Instead, we fuel our desires, and bring them to action through our will. The defender of desire is revitalized and ready to challenge all comers in battle.

---

[8] Collins, *Light on the Path, supra*

Will

The apparition of the angel of Mary taught that men must set aside their ways of will and desire. We know about desire. But what of will?

Mind acts through its will. Will is the means by which desires are fulfilled. It is the sword with which the mind fights in conflict with the desires of others. It is the way the mind imposes its desires upon the world. What the mind desires, the will fights to get.

The will sees any action that does not conform to the mind's desire as an attack on the very essence of its existence. It reacts quickly, both defending and mounting a counterattack. A fierce fighter, the will takes any action at hand to prevail unless subdued by the mind. For none can harness it but the mind. None can unleash it either. Will is a wild beast whose spirit can be broken but never tamed. It knows only domination, or to be dominated. For will, there is no other way.

Thankfully, mind retains the key to halt the will's bloody march through the world. This key is to lose desire. Without desire, the mind has no need to send forth its legions. Without desire, the will has no victory to pursue. Without desire, the will roams the land like an invincible warrior that has conquered all its enemies. Without direction or enemy to fight, it will wither until it is no more. But until desire no longer rules our lives, we must shackle our soldiers with self-restraint and forbearance to insure they keep the peace.

Desire motivates the mind to create the world in which we live. It inspires us to achieve, to build, and to dream. It is the mechanism by which we apply thought-energy to bring image into form. Similarly, through its reverse, the dream begins to unravel. When we set aside our desire, we free the mind to apply its thought through meditation to build a portal between the worlds.

Losing desire is like peeling an onion. Layer by layer we leave our desires behind, until only the greatest are left. Then, with superhuman effort we overcome the last of them, and they are gone. Nothing more holds us to this world. We renounce all, and all becomes ours. We become the selfless servants of the Creator, working only to bring the ways of light into the world.

Attachment to objects of pleasure blocks the path. If you walk it, then break that attachment. Lose your desire. It is the only way to reach your destination.

Construct the Temple

There are so many attributes we reflect that block the light before which our souls call for us to stand. Those who climb the path to awakening should diligently work to overcome these attributes, resisting their expression and creating the habit of performing their positive counterparts. Here are a few thoughts on how to construct the temple in which you will meet your God within.

Do Not Crave What is Not Yours

Have you ever coveted something that belonged to someone else? Perhaps it was lusting after a handsome man or beautiful woman. Or maybe it was jealousy over another's money, job, house or objects of pleasure. Whatever triggers it, such craving feeds an insatiable desire for more than the gifts that are bestowed upon you, no matter how great or meager they may be. This avarice is the spawn of discontent, wrongly whispering in your ear, "The grass is greener on the other side of the fence." But we do not live on the other side. We live where we are, here and now. We can strive to better it, but when it comes at the expense of others, we move farther away from the light.

This is the mental side of theft; such cravings often drive us to take what we want, even though it belongs to another. Fight desire's entreaties to seize for yourself that which is not yours. It is difficult enough to walk the path with your eyes on what you have not, and well nigh impossible when your cravings drive you to act against others.

Though the laws of man carry their own penalty to be paid in this life, the laws of God carry the weight of karma you will carry for lives to come. Free yourself from the spell of desire until the inner mechanism of your discontent is finally resolved. Forbear from anything resembling wanting that which does not belong to you, until the habit of coveting is broken. Allow the light to seep into your every pore, strengthening your intention to move ever closer to its source. Above all, fight the craving that calls out for you to act. For it is a trap you will surely find hard to escape.

Right Observance

Right living. Right thought. Right action. Think only that which creates, aligns, or heals. Replace negative thoughts with positive ones. Use the force of habit to build your foundation. Cultivate only those habits that create, not destroy.

Observe your faith, especially in the light within. Practice it religiously. Make it part of your life, and allow not a day to go by when you do not put it to work.

Let there be no mistake about how to share the love that comes into your heart. Be kind – in all things, in all ways. And do good things in your life. Let your actions reflect your love for the world.

Most of all, make a mark. Contribute to society. Leave the world a better place when you go.

Character

Character matters on this journey, for it is the quality of each soul that is tested before it gains admittance to the kingdom of Heaven. Cultivate the best you find in each man; seek and cast out from within you any hint of that you despise in others.

Hold the highest ideals clearly in your mind, and live as if you have already achieved them. You are already perfect inside. You only have to let it out for all the world to see.

Purity of Thought and Deed

Think no evil. Do no evil. These are key. Strive to remove all impurity from your life. Be impeccable in your thoughts and deeds. Your efforts to purify the bodies are wasted if you reintroduce contaminants through wrong thought or action. Diligent effort is the key. Do not be dissuaded when you fall off the path, nor chastise yourself for your failure. That is just excess baggage that will weigh you down. Just take note of where you are and what you must do, then begin again. The road is long, and you will need all of your energy to succeed. Do not allow it to dissipate through self-abuse.

Be Content

Life's greatest challenge is to be content. Contentment is an inner condition that reflects our acceptance of God's will. It is life without allowing desire or expectation to motivate thought or action. Contentment is the foundation of inner peace.

Yet who is truly content when not aligned with the soul?

Our lives are filled with the chase of desire. We work to get more money so we can buy a bigger house or a nicer car that will drive us faster or allow us to feel the wind in our hair. We look at what we have and want something more or different. Even our bodies are lacking. Sometimes we even want the people in our lives to be different than they are. Want drives our world. Desire breeds more desire. It also brings discontent.

Even those who walk the path are not content, for their discontent drives them to make the transformation. If they were comfortable where they were, they would not be called to awaken. Therefore the task before them is to somehow be content in the process of awakening, and take heart that by continuing the process, the result will ultimately be theirs as well. At least the seeker of light recognizes the hazards desire places before him along the path and how to overcome them. Those not yet underway are not so fortunate.

Desire pushes us over the edge of our ability to control ourselves. More. Better. Bigger. Or whatever may strike our fancy for a new sensation. Desire urges us onward, and if we slip, it takes us right over that edge into addiction.

Addiction. The word conjures up images that make us shudder. Pictures of dirty needles and lives lost in the gutter fill our minds. The opposite of forbearance, it is the manifest inability to control our pursuit of desire. Addiction is by definition repeatedly succumbing to a desire without the ability to stop.

We look down on those who exhibit such tendencies with pity, yet but for the grace of God there go we. All of us are addicts in one form or another – addicted to desire. Unlike the addict of common parlance, our addictions are usually not to a single desire. Instead, we jump from desire to desire in socially acceptable fashion, seeking one then another and on to another. Nevertheless, we are unable to resist, much less control, the call of our desire. Just as one craving is lost or controlled, another springs up to take its place. At other times, they coexist and we chase them all.

We think we can stop at any time, but like the addict, we don't want to stop. They make us feel good. Life is hard enough. What's wrong with desires, anyway? So the craving never ends. Desires fill our thoughts.

Peace comes only by purging desire from our minds, and accepting life as it comes. So long as our heads are filled with its cravings, we are always distracted from where we are. For the circumstances of the moment to be enough, we must focus the attention only on the moment, and cast desire out of our thoughts.

Much like the intermittent attainment of enlightenment, at first you may be able to hold the focus of your mind only briefly. But in that moment you will bathe in the cool waters of the lake of peace. Life will be as it should be. As meditation aligns the bodies, the hold of your desires will weaken, and the moments will grow longer and more frequent. The peace of contentment will sweep over you in waves.

All who incarnate must learn the lesson of contentment. Those who walk the path of awakening will apply the tools to make it happen.

Aspiration and Devotion to the God Within

The inner voice is not only your teacher. It is your soul. It is your Christ. It is the God within. Devote your life to hearing and heeding its call. Worship at its altar. Sacrifice yourself to it, and let nothing stand between you.

Those who seek to awaken must find the light. The still small voice is your guide. Follow its voice, even when you are uncertain. The way is not always easy, and you must be motivated to remain on the path. Do this by lighting the kindling of your growing desire for the light, and stoke its flame into an all-consuming fire of aspiration. Figuratively set yourself ablaze in service of your inner God by intense devotion to the Ishvara, the soul within.[9]

Cultivate only higher aspiration. There must be no other motive. This is the only intent that will suffice. No desire to partake of the pleasures of the material world. No desire to obtain reward for good service. No desire to experience sensation. Not even a desire to attain spiritual advancement will do. You must become without desire to obtain something for yourself.

Those who tread the path must be holy in their intent. They walk this way only to find the God within, and to serve as they are called. They seek not for themselves. Those who harbor a hidden desire for personal gain, no matter how small, will not be admitted to the highest levels of initiation, much less qualify to merge with the Creator.

Service takes many forms. It may be as simple as extending a helping hand to the aged or one in need, or as complex as attempting to reshape the world and guide others to the light. Service may be in government, health, or any human pursuit. But the spiritual warrior always gives homage to the inner voice. It is the inner voice that controls. Whatever it commands, serve it, and you will also serve the Divine Plan as well. This is your purpose in life. It is your mission. It is your reason for living. Do it well.

If you apply what you learn here, you will begin to recognize the voice that is your guide on this journey. Whether you accept and follow it is up to you. But if you intend to awaken, you must bow down in subservience to your inner ruler, for God sits on the

---

[9]Patanjali, *The Yoga Sutras* from Bailey, *The Light of the Soul*, supra

throne within. He guards the vortex through which you must pass if you are to enter into his Kingdom. Your only aspiration must be to serve Him, and through that service, to fulfill your role in the Plan.

Spiritual Reading

Even though the voice of the stillness is your guide, you have much to learn, and if you let it, it will lead you to that which will help you on your journey. Information must be uncovered, digested, and put into practice before it becomes knowledge. Your quest will uncover many hints. Cultivate the habit of seeking knowledge for its own sake. Your voice will identify that which helps you toward awakening. It will lead you to that which you must know, or re-learn from prior lives. Read the great texts of the past, and absorb the knowledge from each. Seek the learned among you, and those through whom the masters speak. Find the wisdom in all. Leave no stone unturned.

Attitude

Attitude reflects our relationship with the world. It is the filter of our past that determines how we face the day. It colors our experiences, and shapes our response. Just as our sense of taste is tainted by what we've eaten, our attitude shapes the way we view this moment by our response to the moments that came before. Those moments can leave us breathless with anticipation or leave us with dread as we approach the present.

Life is what it is. No more. No less. It is a walk through incarnation to gather experience and sensations. It is our chance to serve the Plan. If we are lodged in the past, the filter of our attitude will color all that we do and see with the stain of the moment past. The spiritual warrior lives with restrained optimism, bringing energy without distortion. Life is neither rosy and pink, nor gray and dark. The lens must remain clear to provide a crisp image of the world, and of us to it.

The warrior's attitude is neutral, free of the influence of what went before. Joyful, but not exuberant. Lighthearted, but not carefree. Enthusiastic, but not artificial. He does not fluctuate from one extreme to the other; instead, he strives to maintain an even attitude. Life is met with balanced awareness. Neither too high nor too low, the warrior strives to live dispassionately detached from the affairs that come his way to avoid being overtaken by the chaotic swings that mark the impact of the emotional body. Once gone, they too become part of the past.

Take this if nothing else from these words. Greet each day with a smile on your face, lighthearted and eagerly awaiting each new experience life will bring. Do not crease your brow with worry, or turn the corners of your mouth down in a frown. But do not succumb to the opposite extreme of over-enthusiasm. Neither manic nor depressive must you be. Remain centered, and venture forth to one side or another only as necessary to accomplish your work. Attention to such simple thoughts will transform your life.

Recognize when you get off track, and why. Feel how your emotions fluctuate with the energy of your body, and how they try to change the filter of your attitude. And when they do, quickly respond to recover your equilibrium. No matter your lot in life, only you control how you face the day. Exercise that choice wisely.

Breaking Attachment

By now you see how our thoughts and desires bind us to this world. They are reflected in the relationships we build or break. They show up in our interests and activities, and in the comforts with which we stock our lives. They feed our fears. They even shape our personalities. None who enter into this plane are spared from their attack. But all can reverse their influence.

But why would we want to? After all, these thought-desires bring the world to life. They give it meaning, albeit an artificial one. They give us motivation. And they can make it fun.

Desire's effects are not always so pleasant. They also bring unhappiness, fear and loathing. They bring injustice and deprivation. Not to mention so many of the qualities to avoid, like emotional swings, untruthfulness, theft, avarice, and assertions of will. Then of course there is the greatest reason of all – they bind us to the dream that clouds our eyes.

You stand in the dark at the entrance to a path that holds the promise of a glorious new life. You can see the light from its glow. But you cannot go there. You are caught in a giant spider's web, immobilized by thousands of silky strands, invisible to all but the closest inspection. These strands are the attachments formed by your desires. To an observer, you appear stopped of your own volition. No matter how hard you struggle, the web will not release you.

To walk the path, you must first sever the attachments that hold you in place. Together they are unbreakable. Upon examination, you see the mass of threads holding you in place. You follow one back to its source, where you release its bonds. Then, directing your attention to the next, you begin again. Some are not as easy others, so you move on. You will return for them later. No matter your effort, so many remain. But you persevere, cutting each in turn.

Many are so fine that they are invisible to your eye, no matter how closely you look. You know you are bound, but cannot tell by what. You look, but do not see. Then a stranger walks by with lantern held high, illuminating the path. There, in the reflection of its glow, you see the glint of your bonds. He smiles and walks away, while you work feverishly to cut them. But soon his light is gone, and you can find them no more.

Soon another comes along, and by his light you see a few more strands to cut. And so you hurry to cut them before this light, too, is gone. Darkness again falls over you, and your work is slowed. Then the realization hits – why not light your own lamp by which to work? As you do, its soft glow glistens off the threads, and you can work in earnest now. One after another, you go about your work. First one arm is free, then another, then the legs. Now you can walk the path.

You, too, are bound by desires, thoughts, and other attachments. Hints from this book or other sources are like the travelers that pass by. They can tell you what to look for, and even suggest where to find them. But it is up to you to root them out. And only you can break them. Your light comes from inside, and by its glow must you work. Until lit, you cannot complete your struggle for freedom.

Even with the light, you can never see so long as your eyes are tightly closed. Then again, you may not want to see. The cocoon around you is so beautiful and tightly spun that you may choose not to leave. If you are still caught so in the reverie, I say enjoy your slumber. But if you are ready to awaken from your dream and look about, search out the attachments that bind you. Unleash the sword of your will through your intention and turn it upon the creations of your desire.

This is not to suggest that you need put behind you all that you hold dear. Sometimes much of it will remain, even after you break the hold it has over you. However, if you are to pass, you must choose between desire and the light. You will face this choice countless times until your desire is gone forever. Sometimes you will choose desire. But as the light within you grows, you will begin to release your desires. One by one you will sacrifice them on the altar of light. First will go those to which you are least attached. Ultimately, though, you will renounce something of great value. It may mean the loss of your personal reputation, joy, a life of love, or even your higher aspiration itself. In whatever form it comes, this renunciation marks a turning point in your life on the path. For this is the moment you turn away from the dream to face the light of the spirit. Nothing less than your sacrifice to the Divine Will is demanded before passage will be granted.

Understand this. The way of renunciation and breaking attachments is not easy. Your pain will be great. But when it is gone, you will be free.

> *Before the eyes can see, they must be incapable of tears. Before the ear can hear, it must have lost its sensitiveness. Before the voice can speak in the presence of the Masters it must have lost the power to wound. Before the soul can stand in the presence of the Masters its feet must be washed in the blood of the heart.*[10]

---

[10] Collins, *Light on the Path, supra*

Overcoming Emotions

Emotions are chaos in action. They take us up. They bring us down. They make us happy. They make us sad. They turn us inside out.

All emotions are temporary. They come. They wreak their havoc, and then they're gone forever, leaving behind only their trail of destruction. Emotional outbursts set the etheric body to vibrating, which in turn causes the dense physical body to respond. Strong hormones like adrenaline are released into the bloodstream, causing blood pressure to rise, and heightening anxiety in a fight or flight response. Then they go, leaving behind a body trembling in shock.

It is not just the physical body that is left quaking in the wake of emotions. The mind, too, can find itself bombarded by unproductive thoughts. While the mind is usually a moderating influence on the emotions, these amplified thoughts can paralyze its normal function and cause it to get caught up in the chaos of the moment.

Worse, it can be pushed aside and out of control, as if it were an outsider looking in. When the emotions take control, the mind's point of consciousness leaves the body, usually moving its perspective to the left and above the physical body. When this happens, it is reduced to little more than an impotent observer, unable to exert influence over either the body or the emotions. Devoid of the mind's protection, the body is at the mercy of the emotional turmoil.

Witness extreme rage from anger. The emotion feeds on itself. As it gains force, it can result in violent acts against those to whom the rage is directed. At such times even the taking of a life is possible. Those under its influence are truly unable to control themselves, since at that moment the mind is outside the inner core of the body where the emotions are in control.

This does not excuse, condone, or justify such loss of control to the emotions. Each of us has a responsibility to the others in this world to avoid doing harm. Maintaining control is the only way to insure this. Unfortunately, this is easier said than done, even when the desire to assert such control is present. Understanding is the first step toward its mastery. To gain this, we must first know how the emotions operate, and from where they come.

The difficulty with understanding emotions, much less controlling them, is that they do not operate on the same basis as the mind. Free will is not involved, for emotions are not conscious acts (although intentional acts can trigger them). They are reactive responses to stimuli. They stalk us, silently lurking in the shadows, waiting for their moment to strike.

During emotional attack (attack is the best way to describe it, for it is indeed an onslaught upon the mind and etheric body, bleeding over to its manifestation in the physical body), the aura of the emotional energy field begins fluctuating wildly. These vibrations are often amplified by the mind's incessant dwelling upon the subject of the emotional stimulus. Thoughts replaying the stimulus (the mind-stuff, or *chitta*) run through our heads, acting as kindling that stokes the fire of greater upset. They feed on each other, generating secondary emotional responses like worry or anger, which in turn bring more and greater discordant vibrations.

The key to moderating, and eventually controlling, emotion is to understand the interrelationship of thought with the emotional/physical/mental cycle. If the emotional response is disrupted at any point in the cycle, it will dissipate. Those seeking to understand emotional moderation and control would be wise to examine ways of doing this, among which are: a) attacking the emotional side itself by trying to suppress the emotions; b) controlling the body's physical response; c) intercepting the stimulus before it can generate a response; d) disrupting the thought process which feeds the emotion-generating machine; or e) removing the desire at the root of the thought.

Expectations

Where
Would we find our anger
Without expectations
Of others
Or us?

Suppressing Emotions

Suppressing emotion is both difficult and dangerous until occult energetic alignment is attained. While possibly effective in the short run, such efforts can lead to greater and greater outbursts in some cases, and insanity in others as the emotions fight back to gain their release. Thus suppression is not recommended at any level.

Controlling the Body's Response

Since the emotions work directly upon the etheric body, the body must respond unless some intermediary force (i.e., the mind) intervenes to save it. Without the mind's capacity to moderate the process, the body is at the mercy of the emotions. No control of the breathing, heart rate, perspiration, or other bodily functions can be accomplished unless the mind charges back in mid-attack to help. At best, once the mind steps back into the picture, it can attempt to regain control of the physical response after the emotional attack has begun, thereby to moderate its unsettling effect and avoid greater consequence. This approach is much too reactive for effective use by those seeking alignment.

Intercepting the Stimulus

There is an interlude, however brief, between the stimulus and the emotional response. A practice of observation, called mindfulness, can assist in this effort to recognize the emotional stimulus and act to quell the uprising before it strikes.

Mindfulness is the practice of remaining aware of all things at all times. Its use in emotional control requires constant vigilance. The mind must exert continuous effort to remain attentive without getting caught up in activity, since preoccupation impairs the nimbleness it needs to respond quickly to unexpected situations. Mindfulness juxtaposes the mind's attention so that it can instantaneously recognize the stimulus, and intercept the emotions before they can generate a response. The mind acts a buffer between the stimulus and the response. It tries to recognize when they are about to respond and act quickly to stop them, or at least to keep them from getting out of control.

As can be imagined, this approach is extremely difficult for even the most disciplined aspirant. The time to recognize the stimulus and prevent the response is minimal, and the mind cannot stray for even a moment. As we know, even the most insignificant event can trigger an emotional reaction (whether anger, sadness, or joy), and they can occur at any time. With even the slightest loss of attention or hesitation to intercept, the emotional response will still result. However, mindfulness will still allow a quick response to help clean up the mess and restore normalcy. Even though mindfulness allows us to recognize the situation as it happens, we still need other means to assert control when an emotional response begins.

Interrupting the Thoughts

Mindfulness carried to the next level brings awareness of our own thoughts, and then interposes the will to change those thoughts and avoid the unwanted emotional response. It allows a longer period of response, as well as reducing the impact when emotions attack. Now the mind is alert not only to outside triggers, but also to internal ones, and the interaction between the two. Such a level of attentiveness greatly increases the chances of success, at least for those who are able to do it continuously. Nevertheless, the practice leads us to an important new principle in the battle for emotional moderation.

We all have experienced times where our "thoughts run away with us." The mind is so active that it foresees danger around every corner. However, by monitoring our own thought processes, we will begin to recognize the thought patterns that bring about emotional upset. Following recognition, we can redirect the mind's attention away from the discordant thoughts to some other, more neutral or pleasant object of concentration.

Since the attack is fueled by thought, it can be intercepted by going to a place of "no thought." It is difficult to immediately switch to a condition of no thought, but we can distract the mind and redirect it to a new thought through a process we call one-pointed concentration. This could be some task at hand, or a selected meditation activity in which we can quickly become absorbed, such as following the breath as it enters or leaves the nostrils. As attention concentrates in the new object, no place will remain for the offending thoughts that act as the emotional trigger. Harmless thoughts will replace harmful ones. Soon thereafter, the emotions (being temporary disturbances anyway) will soon pass, and we can go on about our business.

This concept is significant for the aspirant. The mind can only hold one thought at a time. It can be replaced at will. The aspirant can learn much by further considering this subject, and how to replace destructive thoughts with constructive ones.

Removing the Source

Emotional outbursts destroy our equilibrium, and disturb the quietude of our hearts. Only when we are free of desire can we avoid their sudden attack. For too often emotional outbursts result from our inability to attain desires. Greater desire brings greater response. Sometimes that desire is for pleasure or personal attainment. At other times it can be as simple as to remain free from outside influence or attack upon one's person. Desire for ideas to be accepted, to control another's actions, to acquire or perhaps just to not lose something we value, can similarly trigger emotional response.

As but one example, consider desire at the heart of anger. Anger is an emotional defense asserted to protect a desire for a particular result. Release the desire and the need to respond with anger should dissipate.

If emotions are truly to be tamed, we must aspire to release desire, and thereby free ourselves from the karmic cycle and all the emotional baggage it creates. It requires complete remaking of the personality through cultivation and purification of the mind, emotions, and physical body. It means rebuilding ourselves from the ground up.

Desire cannot be tamed in the heat of the emotional moment. It must be attacked long before the trigger is pulled. It is impossible to squelch desire once the emotions are unleashed. Mindfulness allows us to recognize those situations where emotions are commonly released, and then make conscientious effort to withdraw the cause of our potential reaction. Awareness of our inner processes allows us to "turn off" the desire before the emotional reaction can occur, and take whatever steps are necessary to maintain control.

We rise above the emotional roller coaster by carefully cultivating the intent to avoid the desires that put us in situations where emotions can erupt. And when that is not possible, the exercise of our will for alignment helps us intercept and overcome their attack. It is the ultimate exercise of mind over emotion – the mind determines to retain control, and takes whatever steps are necessary to accomplish that. It is only our ability to insulate the tinder of our desires from the spark of emotion that separates us from the insanity of the moment by the mind's pre-emptive strike to assert its dominance. By its use we can say to the emotional beast, "Do what you choose. I will not respond."

The weapon of choice in this battle is meditation. Meditation is the means by which we gain control over the instrument of the mind. Meditation cultivates a stillness that cannot be disturbed by any force, as if a deep lake whose depths remain calm though the surface is rippled by the storms of emotion. When this is attained, the mind will remain still and emotions will be conquered once and for all. It will then be ready to assume its role in our awakening.

This is the condition to which we must aspire. Only then can we hope to move beyond the chaos of emotional response. This is the point at which progress toward alignment becomes possible.

Moderation of the emotional response is essential to all who want to walk the path to its end. Awakening requires the alignment of mind and emotions, so that the two different bodies vibrate in harmony with each other, and then in turn with the vibration of the physical body. Only through conscious and conscientious effort can we flatten its swings and transfer control to the mind. By exercising our will to clip its peaks and valleys, we break its stranglehold and lay the groundwork for the work to come.

Moving Beyond the Senses

The five senses, together with the mind, are the instruments of perception through which we learn about this world. They allow us to gather knowledge and interact with others to construct our lives. Through these senses we perceive the people, objects and events that fill our days; without them, we would be like ships passing in the night, unaware of each other's existence.

These objects of our perception fill the world of the dream, where they get caught up in a group mentality, history and culture to perpetuate its illusion of reality. It is not the reality of our existence before birth or after death. The senses know nothing of planes of existence beyond this one. They only know what they perceive. To the senses, the world is created at the time of our birth, and ends at death of these bodies. It is only through group teachings about past events, and conclusions drawn by the mind, that we get a sense of continuity from some earlier time. Together they weave the web of our dream.

This view that life is not as it seems is not new. For centuries the ancient wisdom of the Himalayas has taught that the temporal world of the senses is *maya*, an illusion painted for our consumption. It suggests an underlying truth to the ancient question, "How do we know we are not asleep, merely dreaming that we are awake, and all that is in our world is a creation of our dream?" But the *maya* goes farther than just suggesting that we are in a group sleep. The illusion brings with it a set of rules and structure that make it "real" to those trapped within its bounds. To those caught in the dream, there is no other reality, no other existence beyond that perceived by the senses. However, by understanding the nature of its creation, we can look beyond those rules to escape the illusion. In other words, this is a dream that the dreamer can enter and leave at will in order to access the realities that exist beyond the dream. The *maya* is the dream of our souls, creating a world in which they can learn and grow.

We enter into the dream at birth, and leave it through death. We are taught to see life's phenomena in the way accepted by the society in which we are raised. And we are filled with society's hope for something more after death. These unwritten rules are passed on from generation to generation of spiritual immigrant, wiping clean any memory of purpose or life beyond this perception. We are conditioned to accept the values and beliefs of those already blinded to the dream, to act according to their rules, to think and communicate in their patterns of thought and speech, and to interpret sensory input consistent with the rules they impose upon us. It is no wonder that we attach significance to this illusion, for we are conditioned to do so by all who come before us.

This is not to suggest that we would see past the barriers of the physical world or know beyond the senses if we were denied the indoctrination of society. Such metaphysical abilities are developed only through meditation, except for the few whose mechanisms are innately tuned to other planes or whose organ of sight has developed beyond the capability of the common man. But we would be free of the artificial attachments that society has conditioned us to interpret with and impose judgments upon our world, all of which significantly impair our ability to join with the soul.

Take for example self-judgment. If we did not judge ourselves harshly for failing to abide by the rules of the dream, how long would the walls that now prevent us from loving ourselves continue to stand? We beat ourselves up because we do not meet the unattainable conglomeration of characteristics that society tells us we must reflect. They say we must be thinner or stronger or sexier or smarter or mistake free. Or believe in this god in this way. Or work to achieve a certain amount of money or the stuff it enables us to consume. Or do this or that all because the mores of society say it is so, which mores we have accepted as the standard by which we will judge our own existence. It is no wonder that peace eludes us. It is through this judgment that we forge the chains of attachment to the illusion. We adopt the rules of the dream as our own, and measure all that we perceive through our senses by them. At its most basic level, our judgment is the mind's application of the illusion's rules to that which we perceive within it. Reject the rules, reject the judgment, and we begin to pierce the veil of the illusion.

It is not easy to turn one's back on all that is painted to the mind. To do so requires changing the mind's frame of reference from that of a leaf caught in the whirlwind of life, to that of a dispassionate observer who voluntarily participates in the experience to test himself and take lessons from which he can grow, knowing all the while that it will most certainly end and he will again return to his life of normalcy in the world beyond. Moreover, by diligent effort, we can get a peek and then a direct connection into that world to guide us through the turmoil.

It begins by considering that the objects perceived by our senses are manifestations of the illusion to create experiences with which we can interact and learn. They are but the mind's interpretations of sensory input to create experiences for the soul's journey.

In fact, none of these five senses are even directly perceived by the mind. All are first received by the senses, and then are transmitted to the brain, where they are subjected to the perception of the sixth sense – the mind itself.

Even so, a signal that is received by the sensory organ is nothing more than an anomaly in the natural order of things, a blip in the flow of energy that eventually makes its way to the sensory organ receptors. Items that we see are obstacles blocking the natural movement of light, causing the light to strike the object and be reflected back to the eye. Things we hear are phenomena that set off a sympathetic vibration in the air that travels to the ear; smells result when molecules escape from an object and waft to the nose;

taste is a chemical reaction caused by substances disturbing the natural, neutral condition of the taste buds; and feel comes when the physical body is impacted by pushing on the skin.

Once these disturbances reach the sensory organs, an electronic signal is sent to the brain, where the data is organized and catalogued. The mind then inspects and interprets this data, and gives it meaning. Then, applying arbitrary rules of interpretation established by society, it gives names to the objects for easier recall, classification, and communication with the society.

These standards are not absolute. Though the object creating the sensation may remain constant, its perception can vary depending upon the sensitivity of the organs themselves, as well as each mind's interpretation of the data they send. This can even vary from individual to individual. For instance, color is a matter of perception, and not necessarily an absolute. Red to one who is color-blind may not be red to one who is not. Nevertheless, once each learns to associate the mind's interpretation of the shade they receive as red, it will remain known as red, notwithstanding that each may actually see the spectrum of reflected light differently. Moreover, once individuals begin to compare notes on their mind's observations, labels are assigned that can spread throughout society and be commonly applied to the object triggering the disturbance for reception. Thus grows the common dream as the base of "knowledge" is adopted by society. These interpretations of phenomena become the common knowledge, culture, and rules by which we learn to operate within the dream. In turn, they become self-perpetuating, as each generation indoctrinates those that follow to apply the filters of their minds in the same manner.

Though these factors establish how we will perceive and interpret the data that represents the phenomena, they are still just phenomena. But who can say for certain that they indeed exist? For all we know for certain is the perception of the phenomena. It is this perception that is the dream. Until we can begin to clear the lens of the interpretive mind, we can never be certain what it is that is really being observed, much less that it really exists, and is not some implanted thought or figment of our imagination.

It is through the exercise of our senses that we interact with the *maya* and create attachments to the objects of our perception. This behavior is acceptable. That is not. This sensation is good. That is bad. Each brings with it an emotional charge, and raises within us judgments of how it meets or deviates from the rules of our illusion. With each attachment to phenomena judged positive we build desires; with each that brings negative response come fears. Our senses therefore lead us to create the very characteristics that stand in the way of unity with our souls.

These attachments are not reality. They are creations of the mind to allow us to hold on to sensations after they are gone. They, too, are the *maya*. In the eyes of the watching soul, there is no *maya*. There is only reality, for it sees without the filter of the mind. Until the path of awakening is completed, the mind cannot know whether the very people, things, and events that result in the sensory input are any more real than the maya of a dream directly implanted into the mind, bypassing the senses while tricking the mind into believing it is real.

The Flower Wakes

Like a flower awakening to the dawn
I greet the silence within
Spreading the petals of my mind
To bask in the light
That patiently shines
In my soul

To prepare for unification we must go beyond the senses to where the dream no longer exists, where its rules no longer apply. We must turn off the mind's incessant interpretation and judgment, and if necessary the very senses themselves, so we can finally arrive at the truth that lies behind the curtain that is draped over our eyes.

Come, look beyond the façade. Do not get caught up in the dream, for though it seems real to those within it, those who can see beyond it know it binds them not to its rules. Break all attachment to the objects of sensation, and the resulting desires will melt away. You will stand at the threshold of the world from which you came, and to which you will return. You will be ready for unification with your soul, and with it to gain the knowledge needed to serve in this world for the benefit of the next. Through your service all planes of existence will be raised – not just the world of the dream. And through your efforts to spread the light, the fog will slowly lift so you can return to the Creator from whence you came.

Meditation

Meditation is the plow with which we turn the inner soil. It prepares us to receive the seed of transformation.

So much can be said about meditation. Libraries are filled with books on its different aspects, but such complexity is unnecessary. For the greatest benefit comes from its practice, and not the method. This cannot be overly emphasized. The importance of meditation for those who consciously travel the path of light is not what you do, but just that you do it. Regularly and consistently.

Many self-proclaimed masters (what is mastery, anyway, but the ability and perspective that come from being a little farther ahead on the path?) would have their followers practice prescribed exercises for specific duration and frequency. And this is all well and good. But understand how that came about. Historically, if a particular exercise or method of meditation tended to bring about some desired condition, it was passed from master to student. And coming from the master, the student took it as law. So the student made it part of his practice, and passed it along to those he taught.

What guarantee is there that this exercise generated the same result in all who practiced it? Or that some other exercise would not as effectively contribute to a similar condition? Most importantly of all, what if that exercise was not appropriate to the student's point in evolution, and therefore inappropriate to his particular needs? Though we all walk the path of light at various stages and degrees of consciousness, we are each unique. One size does not fit all.

So how is one to tell what is appropriate for their place of development? How do they know what their needs are? The answer is easy, yet hard at the same time. We are caught in a paradox. The soul knows what kind of meditation we need, but we cannot hear the soul until we are properly conditioned by the regular practice of meditation.

This Gordian knot is easily cut. Just do it. Meditate in any way or place you feel comfortable. At any time you can. As you do, you will settle into a rhythm that works for you. And its effects will slowly seep into your life.

First, you will notice yourself a little more relaxed as you begin to allow the stresses of the outer world to pass you by. Your ability to concentrate will grow. You may even find yourself becoming more tolerant or loving toward others. These simple rewards alone are more than enough reason to continue. But the major changes are still ahead!

Meditation has a cumulative effect that cannot be measured in the short term, not even by the physical, mental or emotional benefits that are so easily seen. For meditation works on the body's energy field, gradually adjusting those energies so they flow more smoothly. This provides a catalytic effect that combines with the internal work of cultivation to advance the inner transformation at a speed and intensity that can never happen solely by one without the other. But meditation brings about a result even more important than this.

We spoke earlier about the need to live in the moment, and how the soul acts through the now. Meditation allows this to happen. For meditation at its core is simply experiencing the moment. Whether that experience focuses attention on the breath, or whisks us away through some visualization process, when we meditate we allow the mind to release its attachment to the thoughts that usually carry us away. Thoughts may play an important role in our experience of life, but distract us from the present moment. Meditation allows them their leeway, but always returns concentration to the point of attention. It gives perspective and brings understanding how the mind is a tool to be consciously used, and not allowed to run about on its own.

If you choose to meditate, you may therefore find it helpful not to cloud your intention with the desire to accomplish anything in particular. Instead, use the moments of your silence to simply experience the joy of the moment.

Can you allow yourself the freedom to enter into a meditative state unbound by rules, methods or intent? Or are you more comfortable with an externally imposed structure? Above all, know thyself.

If it is structure you need, or know not where to start, I could tell you to sit straight with eyes closed, hands folded in the lap while breathing slowly and deeply, and focus only on your breath. Watch it come in. Watch it go out. All without moving or trying to control or influence your breath. But I will not.

I could also tell those who are more visually oriented to sit quietly and picture they were in a beautiful garden, surrounded by beautiful flowers and flitting butterflies. The scents of gardenia and jasmine fill the air, and a cool breeze lightly brushes your skin. I could also tell you to notice the ball of light that descends from above you in the sky. I would tell you the particular color to use, too, but that doesn't really matter, because you have one already in mind. Or no color at all. And I could tell you to bring that light down through the top of your head, and allow it to spread like a warm liquid throughout every pore of your body before allowing it to slowly flow out of your body down to the center of the earth. And then how the light returns through you, ever so slowly, on its way back to the sky. But I will not.

No, I will not tell you to do anything at all. You may do any of this, or whatever else that comes to your mind. Or you may do nothing at all. For doing nothing is the essence of meditation.

But if you do choose to bring meditation into your life, I hope you also choose to do it with all of your being focused on that moment, squeezing every ounce of life out of the experience.

Trust yourself. You will know what to do. Discover the mastery that is already yours.

The Light

I have alluded throughout this work to the light. It is that light that shines in us through our souls, and that sets into motion the forces that flow through the universe. It is the light that is the source of spiritual will and intelligence, and the power to bring its plan into form.

This book is about your journey to this light. Cultivation is just the means to get there. You seek the light through your soul, which is but a glimmering aspect, but an integral part nonetheless, of the light of the Source from which it came. In an esoteric sense, there is no difference. For the light within the One is the light within the All, and within the Source as well. In Christian parlance, the light is the Holy Spirit, Christ and God wrapped into one. It is the Word that existed in the beginning, and the form that drove away the darkness.

You are encouraged to seek that ray of the light that is within you, so that with it you can merge and become one with the light of all there is, was, and will ever be. Use it to strengthen and guide you, and call upon it to protect you in your times of trouble. When uncertain, turn toward the light, for the light is all that there is. Only there will you find what you seek.

Throughout the years many have spoken of the light. Within the Christian community, the Christ is said to be "Light from Light, God from true God." Just as Christ embodied this light, and lived his life so that all would find it, you, too, must live your life embodying that light. You are the living God that manifests Himself within you and all the other forms that exist within this world. Cherish all as you cherish yourself, and cherish yourself as you cherish all. This is the true lesson of love.

The kingdom of God is within you, and all around you. It is in the rocks and the trees and the birds and the bees. It is in the one you love, and also in the one you do not. Use all of your breaths to find it, and then to make that kingdom a reality in this world of form by all that you think and do. Live as if the light bathes you in its radiance each moment of your life. For it surely does.

Listening to Your Soul

Your soul speaks through your intuition. Meditation facilitates its receipt, though it comes to even those who do not meditate. Most people have experienced it from time-to-time. When it does, we're left amazed once it is gone, not knowing quite what we experienced. Incredulous, we often ask, "Did something really say, 'Watch out'?"

Intuition tunes us in to a higher source of knowledge than we have available through use of mind alone. It describes communication between the mind and the spiritual realms through the soul, upon which the awakened lower mind can draw for direction and guidance.

Intuition is far more than a voice that warns us of imminent danger. It is the hunch that guides our choice when faced with a decision. It is the feeling that helps us sense the intentions of people or situations. Intuition is the voice that guides us back to the path after we have acted contrary to the rules of right living. It is the inspiration of a creative idea that catches our fancy and motivates us to act. And intuition is the flash of brilliance known as insight, when all the stars align and we are given a window of understanding not attainable in everyday existence. Intuition is all of these and more.

Cynicism's pall strains our acceptance of the unseen world. "Why should I listen?" you may ask. Our minds are so caught up in their egocentric view of creation that we deny what we cannot understand, explain, or prove. The existence of a consciousness that lives beyond the bounds of this plane is hard enough to believe in, but to think that something from that world actually communicates with and guides us can shake our beliefs to the core.

We are caught in a tug-o'-war between incredulity and acceptance, with no basis to explain what occurs to us other than the experience it brings. It tantalizes us with the promise of an exciting new frontier, and terrorizes us with the prospect of a power and intelligence far greater than our limited minds can understand. Many therefore shy away from even acknowledging intuitive contacts that represent an unexplainable world that we ignore in hope it goes away.

There is no need to be afraid. There is no need to fear what lies beyond the boundaries of our temporal existence, or shy away when you are at the doorstep of your deliverance. Heaven is calling you. Will you turn a deaf ear?

So often we don't hear the soul speak because our mental chatter drowns out its voice. Cluttered minds drift in and out of reverie, unaware of this force that silently vies for our attention. Intuition cannot guide us while we are deaf to its entreaties. Our deafness remains until we gain control over our inner processes. Until then, its only option is to hit us between the eyes.

So how are you to distinguish the whispers of the soul from the mind's inner workings? The easy answer is that you will just know, but that does not help those who suffer the clutter of a mind run wild. So let us focus on process instead. The soul whispers in the silence, so it stands to reason (something of an oxymoron in terms of intuition) that it might be heard if thought itself were to subside. But as you discovered in meditation practice, this is quite more easily said than done. The mind fights back like a stubborn child. The more we push it to be silent, the more it resists. The intrusive thoughts only seem to grow louder, at least at first.

However, over time the mind can be gently led to understand that it is there to serve us, and not enslave us. Until it becomes a willing and eager participant (rest assured that with diligent effort one day it will), you can watch each thought come and go, as well as take note of the wake it leaves behind. As you do, notice the empty spaces in between. It is in these brief interludes where the intuition will begin to insinuate itself into your field of awareness. As you explore the spaces of silence, you may discern a hint that something invades the silence. It may come as a knowing, a feeling, an unprompted thought, or even an image. Your job is to simply observe, and test it. "Was that for me?" you will think, wondering if it was your soul's soft voice. You will turn it over in your mind, processing and testing it, never quite sure. But as you progress, you will grow more certain, and begin to trust without the mental gymnastics that accompany your first efforts.

This trust is a subjective thing. You will attune to the voice, but attunement does not mean blind obedience. For intuition is not a command, but a suggestion upon which we may act should we so choose after testing for clarity and understanding. And most of all, we should follow it only when it aligns with what we know to be in our highest interests.[11]

Resist the inclination to build dependence on the intuitive flow, for the soul's guidance can be as intoxicating as any narcotic. It is not uncommon to grow so accustomed to its guidance that we wait and wait for direction. The mind grows lazy and drifts away in a fog. The resulting paralysis is as bad as or worse than the clutter with which we began. Intuitive guidance must never become a substitute for our conscious engagement of life. While a valuable resource, it is nothing more than an additional tool to enhance our action and understanding in the everyday world, and must never be allowed to replace reason, feeling, and the exercise of our will.

Notwithstanding the effort to hear it and the challenges it brings once you do, intuitive guidance will greatly assist you on your journey, for it provides the means to set your own heading and adjust your course when you stray. Access it often, and trust that you will hear it. Until you do, work on yourself, lest it decides to remain silent until you are ready to listen.

---

[11] It is important to remember that intuition should never be taken as a directive or a must, but rather a recommendation or suggestion of additional information that we may want to consider. It is much like riding with a back-seat driver. The ultimate decision whether to listen always rests with the one behind the wheel.

The Power of Intention

You cannot step into the light until you first form the intention to do so. Only through your intent will the path appear. It is the intention to change that carries you along the spiritual path. You must intend to reconstruct your Self in the image that is painted for you here. You must intend to find and live in the light of the soul.

Take heed. This simple idea is more than it appears. Careful study and application will demonstrate that intention is a most powerful tool wielded by mystics present and past. Intention is the instrument of change. It is the brush that paints over the old with the image that will replace it. It is also the mechanism by which that image will become the new reality. For what is intended, the awakening soul will try to bring about. This is a lesson that will be driven home time and again on many different levels.

Intention builds the what of creation; it decides what must be done, and causes it to happen. Intention charts the course of life. It determines where we will go when we set out upon our journey, and how we will get there.

Intent is predicated upon purpose. Without purpose, there is no reason to form an intention. There is no reason to even think about acting, much less doing so. So we don't. Without purpose, we will continue to do that which we have already done. Without purpose's guidance, we have no motivation to change of our own accord. In effect, life is a rut, a self-perpetuating habit that once started never ends. It is only once we adopt a higher purpose that we can form the intent to make the long trek home.

To those who seek the light, a higher purpose is sometimes assumed. Yet that purpose may differ even among those who tread the path, depending upon their point in evolution. Some may seek spiritual advancement as a test of will or sense of personal achievement. Others may go out of curiosity. Still others may do it to dispense with karma to avoid future misfortune. And there will be a few who seek it simply to end their cycle of lives. You may begin your journey motivated by one or more of these reasons, but ultimately you will cast each aside, for all who harbor these or similar purposes can never complete the journey of the soul.

By now it should be clear that desire is a chasm that all who traverse the path must cross. Purpose motivated by desire for personal gain, in whatever form it may be sought, only diverts us from the path to sink deeper into the world of desire. Rather than help build a life of virtue and harmony, such desire reinforces our separateness and uses the will to thwart change. Until desire is transmuted into higher aspiration, purpose fueled by thoughts of personal attainment will ultimately deny us our goal. To overcome it, we stoke the fire of service, and play the role written for us in the Divine Plan. This is the ultimate purpose for those who serve.

Purpose keeps us moving in the right direction, and gently reminds us to correct our course when we stray. It reinforces our will when times are hard, and gently urges us onward when our growth seems stopped. It is the standard by which we test all that we encounter on our journey. When we form an intention from higher purpose and determine to see it to fruition, all obstacles magically fall before its might.

The spiritual warrior acts with deliberate intent in each moment, and through his attention brings that intention to life. For attention is the how of creation; it is the kinetic energy of thought-action. Through attention we act, and know not only that we are acting, but also that we create (or destroy) by that action. It breathes life into that upon which it is focused.

The power of intention is manifest everywhere. Without it, nothing occurs. But with it, that upon which the attention is focused will come into reality. If the intention is to create something in the future, then that is what will be created – something in the future. But the future never arrives. The intention must be to create now, or more accurately, to recognize that the abundance about us has already created the object of our intention. We must see it as if it is already created, and believe without doubt that it exists. Then, by pouring the energy of our attention into that image, it will be so. If we see ourselves as already what we want to be, that is how we shall become. It is the greatest of powers on earth. Through it the Creator breathed life into the world.

Intention must be strong, or our attention will waiver. If we diffuse our attention or allow it to wander wherever it chooses, the creative energies are dissipated, and build nothing. The student of the light cultivates an awareness where the attention is focused at all times, and redirects it by strengthening the intention when it goes astray.

The converse of this lesson is equally true as well. Dwelling upon destructive thoughts destroys that which we consider. By thinking we are sick, or ugly, or dumb, or hurt, or poor, or evil, or selfish, or whatever condition we may choose to imagine that is not in accord with what we need to cultivate, then those destructive conditions will become self-fulfilling prophesies. If we think we will never find the light, then the mind will make sure we do not. Therefore the attention must be zealously guarded at all times. Allow no limiting thought to enter your mind at any time. Recognize no imperfection. And see no evil. Cast out anything that does not lead you farther down the spiritual path. Replace them with their spiritual opposite to build the world you seek. Jealously guard your intention to live in the light, and it will serve you well.

If the object of your intention does not materialize, do not give up. Your attention may simply have wandered, you may harbor doubts, or your intention may be divided or weak. Just firm up your intention, and rededicate yourself to its materialization. Appreciate the abundance around you, and clearly visualize that which you want to accomplish. Strengthen it, and again set the goal clearly in mind. Do not give up until it has come into fruition. Only in this way can you make the world to which you aspire.

Intention is the most powerful weapon in the arsenal of the spiritual warrior. Use it wisely.

Belief

Jesus beseeched his followers to believe. Whether it was the withered fig that produced no fruit, or Lazarus rising from the tomb to cast off his rags, belief was always the understated power behind the miracle. It was the answer of his knowing Father that hears all. Ask. Believe with all of your heart, mind, and soul. Know that it will be done.

All things are possible to those who believe. To those who do not, nothing is possible. For belief marshals the forces of light to your cause. It wields the power of the spirit without hesitation, without doubt, without fear, and without agonizing over potential results.

Belief taps the very essence of God's love. It says to Him, "I love you, and I need your help. My channel is open, so send me your love, and make all things right." No father would deny his children that which they need if it is in his power. Especially not the Creator, who gave each of us His power to create.

Belief is not a bet to be hedged, thinking, "Well, I've tried everything else. Maybe this will work." Half-hearted belief is no better than no belief at all. When doubt creeps in, or if you can't feel it, it cannot succeed.

Belief is having the faith that what the mind is set upon will be so. Belief shows your faith that a particular outcome will result from an action. It is wholehearted, and heart felt. There is no separation between you, and the object of your attention. You and the desire become one, and your belief makes it so.

Faith

Faith
In that I do not know
Feeds the hunger of my soul
To taste a world which waits beyond
Feasting
On the words
Of those who claim to see
Their songs of hope
Resonating
With the music of my heart
Casting out all doubt
Their eyes see no more than mine

It is more than a wishful affirmation; it is a knowing in your very core that you cannot be denied. For if you ask, you shall receive.

Rarely is disbelief couched in absolute denial of this power. Instead, disbelief reflects an air of uncertainty, of wanting to be right, but being unable to take that final leap of faith that knows it will be so. So the skeptic pleads, "Show me." But to such a one, nothing less than a miracle will suffice, for doubt is not easily dispelled. Not any ordinary miracle, but one that cannot be explained by the rational mind other than by leaping headlong into acceptance of the Divine. But miracles are reserved to those who believe and act with all of their feeling and faith. Until the Creator's wand manifests desire into form, doubt prevents intention from becoming reality.

When you pray, when you meditate, when you visualize even the smallest of images, do so with all the gusto that you can muster. Put all of your effort, your energy, and your feeling into your work. And above all, your belief. Empower it to be, and allow it to come into creation. See it as if it has already occurred. Rest your faith upon your belief that it is so. And so it shall be.

Faith will move mountains for those who accept the power of the spirit simply because the heart knows it is so. What mountains will you move today?

Living in the Light

On Relationships

So much of our effort has focused on the components of the human organism and how they interrelate. However, no matter how hard we work on ourselves, there are always the others to be dealt with. We cannot walk through life without crossing the paths of many people. In fact, it is our interaction that defines the quality and scope of our existence. Only through others do we learn about ourselves, and implement the purpose of our incarnation.

Man is a microcosm of the universe. Just as we see the lights in the sky as separate stars unrelated to all the rest, we see ourselves as unique beings within the tiny portion of the universe we inhabit, unrelated to the others except by happenstance. Yet our lives are intertwined, just as the stars are merged in destiny with the rest of the universe. All was formed by the flow of light from the great central sun. All are swept by the forces that blow across the world of form. All grow through their relations with the others about them.

It is little wonder that man exists for himself. Man's world revolves around him. His universe is centered in his own consciousness. Each man is a universe unto himself, wrapped in his own unique package of emotions, thoughts and desires that circulate within his microcosm. This egocentrism results not by accident, but by design. Man is literally wrapped up in himself – his energy, his physical body, his emotional body, and his mind. All revolve around the center-point of his own consciousness. Energy flows between the different aspects of our being, pulsing back and forth in a great current of circulation that results in swings between love-hate, joy-sadness, and other pairs of opposites of the integrated personality. Yet no matter its fluctuations, always the perspective of that personality is its center of consciousness, the "me" around which its world revolves.

Like Ships In The Night

Our desires
Pass
Like ships in the night
N'er to meet
In fear of loss
To another's will

This view of creation is more than a critique of the egotistical ways of mankind. It reflects the fundamental nature of our existence, that we are shells of energy swirling about a center of consciousness. This center of our consciousness is hidden from view where none can see but all can find. There hides the soul around which our worlds are truly built; however, its estranged, external shells are blind to this truth. To those shells, the composite lower man, represented by the integrated personality, is a world unto himself, drifting in a universe of vast proportions. Within that universe are the worlds of the others who also inhabit this plane.

Each of us is a tiny world unto ourselves, as if a planet that wanders through its appointed part of the galaxy trying to maintain the equilibrium of its own existence. Too often we are subjected to outside influences that disrupt our delicate balance. Wobbling here and there on their seemingly random courses, we cross the paths of others. When we do, it is inevitable that our worlds will collide.

These collisions result from the interaction of individual wills that seek to give life to their respective desires. From our individual perspective (or more properly, that of the personality), others invade the sanctity of the world we try to build. Though sometimes they act in concert with us, too often they force their desires upon us. We build walls to protect ourselves, reinforcing our feelings of separateness. Those walls just make others work harder to prevail during our interaction, escalating our conflicts. Their renewed attack on our desires is an attack on us as well, for we see no separation between our desires and us. As far as we can see, they are one and the same. So we protect ourselves from attack by attacking in turn. We defend our fiefdoms by slinging barbs and arrows at those who suggest anything even remotely contrary to what we hold dear.

Desire

We color the world
With the brush of our desire
Painting over the canvas
Of those who want another way
While they upon ours paint
Both of us blinded
To that which waits beyond Want's gate

Entanglements with others' desires lead only to conflict. Even when those desires are aligned, the resulting harmony is only temporary until a new desire comes along to replace the old one. When the aligned desires fade, so does the peace. Even so, we should reexamine the points of conflict that crop up between our desires, for it is through our desires that we are taught the spiritual lessons of our lives. They are places for growth where we can learn and test the lessons we've picked up along the way. Unfortunately, while unawakened such interaction is little more than an invitation to wage war and defend the borders of our perceived interests. It is thus that our relations perpetuate conflict. We must therefore always be on guard to overcome this nature if we are to ever live harmoniously with others.

Laws are designed to force us to control our desires and response to others' attacks upon them. Knowing that society frowns on open conflict, we are usually able to restrain ourselves with strangers, and keep our walls strong to avoid being hurt by their "inadvertent" acts. We hold our tongues, and refrain from acting in the face of provocation.

However, we are not so good about controlling ourselves when our guard is down. Around those we care most about, that social restraint is lacking. We don't expect to need it around loved ones, thinking our bond will create an air of civility and understanding. However, we still harbor our desires. They motivate our thoughts and deeds, and spur our will to assert them against even those we love. Without protective barriers and social restraints, our attacks cut to the heart of those who are closest to us; it is also at their hands that we suffer our greatest pain.

The only way to interact for certain without conflict is to focus on desire. If we can somehow let go of desire, harmony will prevail. This is one benefit of walking the path of awakening. As awareness grows, the spiritual warrior becomes ever more aware of the role desires play in interpersonal conflict. With concerted effort, this awareness acts sooner and sooner to end the desire response, until finally there is only harmony within his sphere. At first it may come slowly, but eventually it will come.

The path of awakening allows us not only to exert control over our desires, but also substitute a fervent aspiration to serve the Divine Will for what was once our desire for personal gain. This aspiration is developed as we transform ourselves into a vessel capable of such service. When desire is transmuted into higher aspiration, our focus shifts to the needs of those toward whom our service is directed.

As with all other aspects of cultivation, our relations with others are also guided by the urgings of our souls. Our souls will tell us the way to set aside desire, if we will but listen. It will lead us to find our own center, where the soul's light shines. This same light shines in others as well. Once we find the light within us, we can recognize it in others, too. Then when our worlds collide, we can tune in to the unity we share, and ignore the discordant vibrations as a temporary abnormality that together we must work to resolve. All that is not in accord with the vibration of our souls can be ignored. By knowing ourselves and hearing the voice of the soul, we can weather the storms that rage along the periphery of our interaction.

Our tool to find this light is love. To remove the conflict from our lives, we must show love for others and ourselves as well. Love sensitizes us to the light of the spirit. It heals our hearts and fills us with its warmth from within. It comforts us when we set aside our desires. It helps us overlook the desires of others to find the heart that beats at their core. Love teaches us to focus on the soul within, and not the shell of the personality without. Love recognizes the One Life that is shared by all. Love shows us we are but a single being separated only by our earthly forms. When we see life this way, it is much easier to let the areas of discord pass gently into the night.

Life challenges us to set aside our own desires and use our love to make a difference in the world around us. The soul calls us to serve, and is not in the least concerned with the artificial desires we accumulate in life. To serve effectively we must change our perspective and awaken to those around us, for their lives are intertwined with ours, as ours are tied to theirs. We can no longer see things from within the walls of our desire. If we fail to hear their words or feel their pain, we deny them the gift of our being, and cheat ourselves out of the expression of love their circumstance allows us.

When we wrap ourselves in our desires, we are insensitive to their needs. Do we think we are so important that we can ignore the needs of other beings around us? We who travel the path are no more special than those who share the world with us. Nor are they more special than we. We are all the same. We are one.

The soul will decide our worthiness for unification by the quality of our interactions with others. Only through them can we demonstrate we live the lessons of love that have so long eluded us. Only through our actions can we show our service to the Plan. Those who seek admittance to the world beyond must move gently through life, gracing each soul they meet with love and compassion while setting aside the ways of will and desire.

In the end, we are judged by the lives we touch. This is the great lesson of life. Learn it well, and the keys to the kingdom will now and forever be yours.

Living with Passion

We who are embodied are challenged to bring equal passion to all parts of life, no matter how the lives we lead dictate their demands upon our time and attention. We might increase our chances of meeting the day with unrestrained enthusiasm if we were to simplify our routines. However, modern society frowns upon those who attempt simplification by self-sufficiency or withdrawal from society. Instead, we are encouraged to depend upon complex channels of distribution and commerce to obtain the means for our survival, and the technology developed to make it possible.

Their benefits are hard to deny, at least when judged by the standards of this temporal world. Foodstuffs and clothing arrive at our doorsteps upon demand. Computers store and manipulate large amounts of information in a flash. The Internet has opened channels of knowledge and communication not even dreamed of only a few years before. Telephones allow us to speak instantly to others, whether across the street or around the globe. Through the wonders of television we invite the world into our homes. We surround ourselves with machines to wash our clothes, cook our food, and relieve us of the other necessities of survival. Vehicles that float, fly and roll move us here, then there, all so that we can do more over a wider distance in the same amount of time. This is the modern world of technology and progress.

What Else Is There?

To live
To laugh
To love
What more can we ask of life?

On a fundamental level we have acquiesced to a world where spiritual needs (not to mention the underlying Plan of creation itself) take a back seat to the march of technology. We have tacitly agreed to idly drift through the hazy world of society's spiritual wilderness. It is little wonder we put so little into life, living in denial of our true selves and the reason for our very existence.

We retain the power to choose another life. However, radical changes in direction are difficult. Entanglements of family, friends, work, and societal norms exert their influence to keep us moving along the chosen path. It is difficult to avoid frustration when they fill our days with activities and expectations that leave so little room for us to pursue the needs of our souls. It is even harder to meet those demands with equal passion when resentment, fatigue, and emotional swings exert themselves as well.

Still, no one moment is any more or less special than the next. Each deserves our enthusiastic and undivided attention. Similarly, no person is insignificant, or event that graces our day. They are important, and we should treat them so. We should meet them with wonder and awe in hope of squeezing every last ounce of experience from each. Let us give thanks for the gift they bring, for it is indeed unique, to be cherished for all of eternity.

The lesson is simple. Approach each moment as if it were the first, or the last, of your embodiment; treat it as if it holds the key to all of life's lessons that are to be learned. Breathe the life of your attention into each second of your existence, for that is the reason it was given to you. Wear your passion for life on your sleeve, for where else would you hide it?

This does not mean to endlessly chase your own desires, even if that desire is the aspiration for higher spiritual advancement. Do not turn your back on society, nor your families or responsibilities in the world. To the contrary, so long as you are part of their world, give yourself completely to each and all of them. Not in life-draining slavery to quench their every desire, but to meet their real needs that will grow ever clearer in your new-found sight. For you are a part of them, and they of you.

If you embark upon the spiritual path with serious intent, you will inevitably begin to reorder your life, dropping activities that bring little value, while perhaps adding others that do. It is good that you do so, as long as such changes are made with a watchful eye toward serving the spirit and an ear tuned to intuition. Do not run from your fears, or break one set of attachments simply to create another. When you are faced with a choice, be guided by the light, and share it with all who touch your life. In this way, your hand will be steady and your heart will be true.

Begin slowly. Start close to home. As your passion grows, expand your circle of influence, until all are warmed by its touch.

Apply all the passion you can muster in each moment of your life, and make it so.

Passion's Flower

Passsion's flower
Spread forth your petals
So that I may taste the nectar of your love
And rest in the warmth
Of your embrace

The Tortoise and The Hare

Much ado has been made about the path to awakening, and the cultivation that makes it possible. It is such a solitary path, and so easy to lose one's way. Even the best-intentioned aspirant can work feverishly one day, and then be unable to find the path the next. How do we not succumb to the difficulties along the way?

It may help to consider the race between tortoise and hare. Some who follow the Light are prone to intensive effort, but easily disillusioned when that effort does not generate some perceptible result or sign of advancement. They are like the hare, running swiftly toward the destination but lacking great progress because they tire easily and stop often to rest. Once at rest, the hare quickly grows impatient, its attention darting here then there. Enticed by some new promise of hope or whim, the hare darts off in a new direction, the original path but a distant memory.

Others who walk the path are like the tortoise. They plod along, step by ponderous step. Although it appears they make no headway, slowly but ever so surely they march toward the goal. Unable to see much farther than their feet can take them in the next few seconds, their eyes are firmly set upon the ground. Their intent is not the destination, though its suggestion keeps them moving. Their intent is focused only upon the next step.

The aspirant must cultivate the way of the tortoise. Patience and persistence are virtues that will bring much reward. A single lifetime is rarely enough to reach the light. It takes effort exerted over many lifetimes as one climbs the path. This is not to suggest that our work now is insignificant, for it is only through the patient effort of each lifetime that we travel closer to the goal. Even if our effort in this life is insufficient, will we deny ourselves the steps that we can take now and leave even more ground to cover in our future lives?

Nor does this suggest that we should set aside our shell so we can travel as fast as the hare. The ways of cultivation bring progress as well as danger. There is great risk to those who bypass necessary foundations, rush their training or ignore the cultivation of their personalities and purification of their energy body. The way of the hare is to hurry and wait. It portends danger. Its risks are many.

Walking the path is like trying to cross a wide, swift river by stepping on stones arranged across the stream. The broader your foundation, the more certain your step will be. However, you cannot just rush headlong across, for your chance of misstep grows the faster you travel. Even the gait of those most prepared must not be hurried. Though some of the stones were left for your use by prior travelers, those who lost their way laid others. Be certain where you step, for some of the stones are unsteady and the waters are swift.

Just as you must not cross too quickly, neither must you tarry along the way. The rocks provide no shelter, and expose you to the river at its worst. Your safety is on the other side. Stop too long and your attention may be diverted to the waters of will and desire rushing all around you. If so, you will become disoriented and it will be easy to fall. Those who do will find it difficult to assume the old ways of their lives, caught once again in the raging river of desire while grasping for a hold on the cornerstones of cultivation.

Nor is the way back any easier, even though you have faced its dangers before. Besides, the place from which you started holds nothing for you now but a temporary respite before you again set out across the rocks for the other side. You might as well continue from where you are, because you know you will have to cross them again, and neither the effort nor danger will be lessened in the future.

Once your eyes have seen the far shore of enlightenment, you will be satisfied with nothing less than its attainment. For there the river is calm, and its shore green and lush. But the way can only be traveled one step at a time. Do not grow frustrated if the waves of will and desire continue to wash over you; with each passing wave they will diminish, along with their hold over you. Do not despair if your emotions do not succumb with your mere wish they were gone; trust that with each step you grow closer to their moderation and ultimate alignment. In this way progress will be yours.

Each leap from rock to rock will reveal them for what they are – tests you have not yet passed, carefully crafted to remind you of that which must become part of you. Take your time and choose your steps wisely. Only in this way will you reach your destination.

If you should fall, do not despair; you have not failed, but simply received another opportunity to learn. Little is gleaned from success. It is from life's adversity that we learn best. It is only by sipping the bitter wine of our failures that the nectar of success tastes so much sweeter. Greet each misstep as an experience from which you can grow. You will not find more than that for which you are ready. All that happens is a lesson from which you can learn if you will but examine it and take it to heart.

Become the tortoise. Walk slowly but surely each step of the way. Work always toward your goal, and let nothing deter you. The way must be persistently walked one step after another. Learn this lesson, and you will go far. Success will surely be yours.

Life is a Classroom

Life is not the chance series of events that we envision it to be. It is an orchestrated score that brings together the diversified instruments of all of humanity to play their various roles so we each can serve the purpose and learn the lessons for which we came.

Those who are asleep think there is nothing more than life within the dream. Day after day events happen, some by the conscious planning of the lower mind, some by intervention by others, and still more by coincidence or chance. Since the mind has no ability to see beyond the dream, everything that occurs within it is bound by the rules of the dream. That is to say, all things must perform according to the expectations of the dreamer. The dreamer will only accept that which the rational mind can comprehend and accept. If it cannot be explained to the satisfaction of the mind, it will in all probability be rejected.

We are born into life for a purpose, though the unawakened may dispute even that. This purpose remains obscure until we achieve enlightenment, when the knowledge of the soul becomes known in this world. Nevertheless, underlying the individual events of life is the same reason for being – to learn the lessons experience brings for the growth of our souls, and fulfill our role in the Divine Plan. Unfortunately, not only are we unaware of our role in this Plan, we are quickly diverted from our task by the obstacles life puts in our way.

Little do we know that the events of our self-indulgent lives are carefully designed to present us with lessons to teach us, followed by tests we take through our power of choice. We must show that we have learned the lessons we came to learn; if not, they will be repeated time and again until we do. Our lives are arranged to set up these choices, and through them to demonstrate our growth. First we are taught by being led to the needed ideas and sources of knowledge. Then we are presented with situations to apply the lesson in order to make it part of us, thereby altering our personalities and behavior to incorporate it into our lives. Finally, we are tested, where we show we have learned it. Over and over again the lessons keep cropping up throughout our lives, until finally we either die or learn it and move on.

Sometimes life tests our control over emotions. It may test how we handle suffering. Or it might test how well we apply the laws of love, experience giving, or allow others to experience those lessons as well. However, many of its lessons test our ability to overcome the temptation of our desires. Perhaps you've experienced such a situation in your own life. First comes exposure to things that bring pleasurable sensations, such as drugs, alcohol, or sexual activity. But you know that you should not succumb to the desire to do it again. Next you must choose whether to engage in it anyway. You might choose to resist. But often you don't, and succumb to your desire. Even though you know the activity is not appropriate, you do it anyway, unable to control your desire that has grown into an unquenchable thirst. And so the opportunity for the sensation presents itself again and again, until finally you overcome it in triumph, or submit to hopeless addiction.

Many such experiences are written in our book of life. Through them our souls grow. When we can face the object of our desire, first to experience it, then overcome it, and ultimately to release it, the lesson is learned. The test is not the strength of will to resist the addictive behavior. Rather, it is our ability to recognize and break the attachment to the underlying desire. If we win by merely resisting the behavior by strength of will, the stimulus will continue to reappear; we must continue to resist, for if it weakens, the behavior resumes. However, if we break the hold of desire, we lose the very reason for the addiction itself. As the desire fades, so will the tests. No longer needed, they will fade into the past.

We find such lessons and tests in every part of our lives. They are in the work we do, the places we go, and the people we see. But they are most readily seen in how we interact with others. We continually fall into the same patterns of behavior, asserting our wills against those of others, sometimes with tragic results. Marriage partners fight incessantly over the same old issues, never realizing the real test is not their ability to resolve the issue, but rather their ability to move beyond will and desire so a solution can be harmoniously achieved. Egos get bruised, and personalities get in the way, blinding them to the answer. So they continually fall into the same behavioral traps, and are tested over and over again, each time failing without ever seeing the conflict as an opportunity for growth.

Those who choose to walk the path of awakening will undertake a thorough evaluation of their own personalities, and begin to know what they must do to better themselves. Once the steps of cultivation are known and their importance understood, few who truly seek to awaken will continue to blindly chase their desires and assert their wills, at least without some degree of guilt and self-approbation. No longer can they indulge in fits of anger or contests of will without later chastising themselves for their failure to abide by the commandments. Life is no longer "fun" in the sense of chasing desires. Life is work to demonstrate our learning and to move on to our next hurdle.

We have no reason to condemn ourselves for failing these tests. There is no benefit to speed, only to success. It matters not whether the test is passed now, or many years or lifetimes in the future; only that we learn the lesson so the soul can move on. Of course, the sooner we learn it, the faster our souls can develop and progress along the spiritual path. Moreover, another test will always arise to take its place as the soul moves to each new level of learning required for its development.

Similarly, there are no coincidences, for coincidence implies a chance random occurrence. They are not random, nor are they coincidental. Though we may not understand them, coincidences position us for the tests to come. Even without considering that all things happen according to Plan, the coincidence itself raises questions about its randomness. Seemingly chance meetings often lead to significant relationships, transformations, or opportunities in the future. Shared thoughts independently reached can bring strangers together. A synchronicity of unrelated events involving related people occurs simultaneously in time in separate places. We know they cannot be unrelated, yet because we cannot see the relation, we chalk them up to coincidence.

Each coincidence opens a door that leads us down a new road. We allow ignorance to rule our minds, and deny their significance, only because we cannot see down that road from our perspective in place and time. With hindsight, we clearly acknowledge that the coincidences of our past have led us to where we are today, where we face the lessons of this moment. It is then we know for sure that such meetings are not by chance, but were arranged to bring us to this place in space and time. Each coincidence leads us to new learning opportunities; each should be eagerly anticipated for the new lesson and opportunity it brings.

The spiritual warrior greets each moment as a battle for his soul, recognizing all that occurs is either a new lesson or opportunity to apply that which he has already learned. What lessons have you faced today? How did you respond? What did you learn?

Come From Where You Are

Turn not from your faith, but come from where you are. Your spirit welcomes you with open arms, no matter your beliefs. For the soul speaks not one language of faith, but all. It whispers to us of the love that shines in our hearts, and the love we have to share with the world.

Religion is the form through which faith is taught, along with its underlying principles by which men are to live. It varies from culture to culture. All are right, to where they go. Yet none is whole, for all fail to show the way to complete the journey. Even those whose religion calls them to seek the silence within do not yet see the entire way.

There were some scattered across all the religions who learned the lessons and completed the journey. They have taken their place among the revered wise men and women of their times, and should continue to be held high in the eyes of their peoples. It is unnecessary to list them by name, for they are many and my words are few. They gave their lives to the joy and wisdom that is only found within, and shared the love they received with all whose paths they crossed. This is the lesson we all must learn, and the footsteps we must follow.

None of us can change that which has gone before, for what is done is done. Nor can we change the 'morrow, for that which is to happen has already been written on the walls of the halls of learning. All that we can influence is the now. All that we can change is us. All that we can be is what we are already but do not yet know.

Whatever your faith, whatever beliefs you have accepted as your own, they are of no consequence in your journey to the spirit. You will not be called to give up those beliefs. Nor will you be called to adopt others that are not now yours. You are only called to look within and to find the place of silence that dwells within you. Once you do, the light of love will begin to fill your heart and guide your way.

You will hear the answers you seek from the voice that whispers within, where only you can hear. No one else can show you where to find it. No one else has the answers that are yours. If you look, it will appear. If you listen, it will speak. If you ask for guidance, it will lead you.

Wherever you are, it waits for you. For some, that wait is patient, for others it jumps up and down to get their attention. But no matter your point of beginning, its light shines as a beacon to lead you to the destination. It is your guide. It is your soul.

Heaven, earth, past and present meet in the Now.

Before you is a symbol given me in my training. It may be of help on your journey as well. Commonly known as the Maltese or celtic cross, it has much significance through history, particularly within the church of those who follow the teachings of the Christ. Do not let those teachings distract you. Go beyond the trappings of the religion and explore their spiritual meaning.

At the center is the soul, living in the now. To the left is all that has gone before, and to the right all the possible tomorrows that may rise up to greet you. Above is the world of the spirit, from which the power of love flows. Below are emotion, mind, and the physical body, comprising the three lower bodies of the dense physical world we know. The circle represents the manifested world of incarnation and all the limitations of this plane, beyond which no one incarnate can pass. Yet the plane of the spirit and the tangible world below extend beyond these limitations, representing that the existence of the soul, and indeed the power of all creation, neither begins nor ends with our incarnation in this world. Life is eternal, and it is up to us to open the channels so that the all-knowing power of the universe can flow to us in this world. The soul only lives in the now, and in the now all things are possible. Consider it wisely, for it will guide you when you do not know where to turn.

Again, no matter your place of beginning, the light of the soul is yours if you will but seek it. To find it, though, it asks only that you cultivate yourself through love and compassion, and apply the rules of living that prepare you to receive its host. It also demands that you apply yourself through single-pointed meditation to align and open the channels through which the energy and knowledge will flow. With these simple tools, you can travel from the place of your heritage to the place of your destination – the land of the soul, the world of the spirit, the One, the All, the Source, our God, the light.

Moses and the God of the Jews do not deny you this. Neither do the Christ and his loving God. Nor do Mohammed and the love of Allah. Nor does the Buddha in his simple rules of right living. Each asks you to find the light. Each shows you part of the way. Each leads you to that point of embarkation. But only you can go the rest of the way from there. They stand at the door, shining their light, and pointing you to the road ahead.

Be off with you now, and find the light that shines for you alone.

The Difficult Path

Growth comes in spurts, and can be quite painful as the old ways are discarded and the new have not yet taken their place. During such times you will be exposed, alone, and question your ability to stay the course in the face of apparent hardship. However, though such times may appear harsh, they are necessary moments of enlightenment for those on the path, for they must accept that all things that are to come to pass will do so. The trials and tribulations are tests of your resolve, and are important milestones that must be passed before you will be permitted to taste the fruits of the light.

Atlas

Like Atlas straddling the Straits of Gibraltar
I stand
Anchored both in darkness and in light
Back bent
By the weight of their worlds
Unable to move toward one without dropping the other
All the while
Their battle rages inside my head
No relief to spell me
So that I may be on my way

The light will eventually melt away your attachments to the world, perhaps even leading you to renounce a very personal part of your life. You may deny yourself something as simple as a particular pleasure, or as complex as all that you have or hold dear. However manifested, thus renunciation is an important event representing the sacrifice of your own will and desire to that of the Divine Plan. Your desires are lambs that you must sacrifice to see the true light that burns within.

This may be a painful period, for you will have not yet found that which you seek, but are now denied that which you formerly held dear. Uncertainty reigns. Even though the mind knows that uncertainty is to be cherished as a sign of submission to the Divine will, it still grasps at the straws of its security.

Know that light shines in your heart, even though darkness swirls about. Do not be tempted by worldly things which have previously been beyond reach, or promises of pleasures that are awaiting if you will abandon your journey to partake of life's spoils. Do not allow the dream to intoxicate you. Instead, remain strong, with eyes firmly fixed upon the path.

Though sometimes harsh or obscured by a bend ahead, the path is not a way of deprivation. All abundance is given those who know the ways of the soul. Neither is it a way of personal destruction. It is a way of hope and promise, to give knowledge of the purpose for which you were born, and the meaning for existence you seek. The path shows you how to step beyond the cycle of karma and reincarnation to serve the Creator as you were intended to do. Walking the path will give you inspiration and insight into life that you would otherwise be denied, and tap into intuition's absolute knowledge that awaits beyond this plane of existence.

Let go of that to which you cling so tightly, and trust that what you need will remain, so that your hands will be free to grasp that which is coming in your life ahead. If you hold on too tightly, you can gain nothing further, and will be denied the fruits of the life you long to create. If you get too caught up in the dream, you will be unable to enter the world of the soul.

Letting go is so difficult. It brings pain. It brings sacrifice. But it also brings reward, knowing that the future is more than the temporary life before you. The future is the great eternity from whence you came, and to which you will return after this stint in the world is concluded. Letting go sets the stage for the ultimate of personal attainment through union with your soul.

Whatever it is that you grasp so tightly, loosen your grip and set it free. If it is needed for your journey or the enlightenment of those whose lives you touch, then it will remain yours. If not, it was nothing more than dead weight that will no longer slow you down. Your spirit will be brighter and your step lighter as it passes into the distance.

Be brave. Be firm. Be strong. You are the captain of your ship, the master of your fate. You choose to hold on to the world that you have created. You can choose to let it go as well. The rewards you will reap will be greater if you will trust in the great unknown, and take the leap of faith required for all who would walk this way.

When in doubt, decree to your voice within, "I am the strength that sets down this weight, and cuts the chains of attachment as I walk along the way. I am the wisdom that knows that which will not accompany me, and the compassion that lends a helping hand to those who remain behind until they too can see the light."

Decree that it is so. And so it is.

I Walk But Once

I walk but once along this sand
Waves lapping at my feet
My footsteps gone, no trace behind,
The past I can't repeat
I struggle to remember
The days my eyes did greet
Now but a distant haze, not so unlike
Where earth and heaven meet

Some come to walk beside me,
For a while at least today
We talk and laugh together
And watch the children play
But soon their time is over,
I journey on alone
Their faces now but memories,
Shadows all but gone.

Step by step I wander
To nowhere I do fear
Then suddenly it hits me,
My purpose now so clear
For oh so long I've struggled on
Not knowing where or why
So simple was the answer,
Bright as the sunlight in my eye

Wet sands squish between my toes
Wind whispers in my ear
Warm rays of sunlight on my back
Birds laughing in the air
God's beauty's all around us
His love casts out my fear
I thank the Lord I noticed
And that I still do care.

Reflecting on my life gone by
Who knows of days to come
No more, no less, I face my fate
Accept what I've become
So bright and clear my vision
So simple in my quest
To live, to love, and share my life
And give my very best

It matters not the journey
Or the burden I must bear
For what's inside is all that counts
And how it I will wear.
The task is mine to face alone,
This walk upon the beach
And let the light I feel within
Warm all within my reach.

Afterword

I am every man, yet I am no man. I am with you always, yet we have never met. I am the source of your strength deep inside, where you never let anyone enter. And I am part of you, just as you are part of me.

I am to you both man and woman, father and mother, son and daughter. I am your lover, and you are mine. I accept you as you are, because you are you.

Yet, I am also your conscience, the whispering voice that no one can hear but you. I am the music that fills your soul, and the light that shines in your heart. I dream your dreams, and bear your hope for tomorrow. I am your teacher, your adversary, and your friend, and you are mine.

Still, for all that I am, I am nothing. I am the worst of all men, the darkness that hides deep inside, hopefully never to see the light of day. I am your temptation and your desire. I am your heartache and your tears. I am lower than the dust of the earth. But together we are whole, we are love, we are mankind, and we are God in all his glory.

There is naught that I can say that you have not heard so many times before. Accept it or not, the choice was always yours, as it remains so. The words are but reminders of that which you already know. All truth is yours if but you will turn within.

Yes, we are tempted by the world that greets us, eager to meet our every desire. Each desire brings one greater, addicting us to our own pleasure and the reverie it weaves. See desire for what it is, and wield it wisely, for too often we are blind to how our desires strike the hearts of those we love, and who love us. If you must experience that desire, then quickly let it go. Let not it keep you from the truth you must seek.

You will be judged by the choices you make. Yet, the judgment that will be heaped upon you will be harshest from the voice that only you can hear, at least when you will listen. Remember, it speaks for you – it is your true guide. Listen and heed.

When you err, beware the walls you build inside that block out the light. Let not your fortress become your prison. Do not allow your fear of the dark to deny you forgiveness from the most important one of all – you!

And when life goes not as you wish, and your choices do not always seem right, remember that things have a way of working out. That is the way. It is so written.

You may not see me, but I will be there, waiting in the shadows. When you are in need, I will hear your call. Even if you cry out by only a thought, you will not suffer alone. My spirit will be there to hold your hand and show you the way.

I will not judge you, for I love you the way you are, as I hope you will learn to love the world around you. Look about. See the others whose paths you cross. Dwell not on their blemishes. See them as perfect, too. Love them, for though they appear different, I am part of them as well. As you are, too. We are all the same. We all love and laugh and hate and cry. We fear and hope and pray. And we all share the light, even though some may see it more than others. We are many. And we are one.

So as you read this, think not of yourself, nor of me. Think of everyman, for there in him go you. Each man is the mirror of every other, reflecting that which we choose to see. Cherish their differences, for they are gifts to allow you a view into your own soul.

Treat well this world in which you live, and the body in which you ride. Life is a wonderful gift. Enjoy it. Be joyous. But always strive to remain dispassionate to this incarnation, for it, too, is but a dream that will fade when this life is gone, while your soul will journey on.

And when the day is dark, look within. Find the light inside where love dwells. Bathe in its glow. Live in the moment, and let the past and future merge in the distance. The now of the light is what you seek.

Find it, and you will know. Look. Listen. And love. For love is the way.

Go with love!

A message from John:

Take the Next Step

My friend:

You have come so far. Not just in the inner exploration that was perhaps accelerated by reading *Whispers in the Silence*, but your journey along the evolutionary path of your soul through this and other lives.

I do not know if that journey has yet allowed you to glimpse the perfection that you are. If not, know that I see it, and hold for you a vision of that mastery and all the possibility it offers your world.

We cannot predict the experience of life. It brings what it brings; our job is to deal with it yet still stay on course. Even the intent to steer in a particular direction may not be enough to overcome the obstacles that derail us along the way. They can cause us to throw our hands up in frustration, or worse, to give up our effort to align the outer form with our inner image.

This difficulty getting – and staying – on track is not unique to any particular place along the way. Nevertheless, even knowing the path grows wider with every step does not make it any easier to travel. At times we are all tested by what life brings. Each experience brings another piece needed for the growth of our souls.

Yet this effort is often exhausting, if not exasperating. It is important to rest, renew and rededicate ourselves to the journey so we do not succumb to the winds of fate.

As a result, I created a space where people can gather strength and guidance to take their next step. After all, that next step is what faces each of us. Sometimes it is as simple as appreciating the people and world around us. At other times it takes every ounce of our determination just to face the day. Whether easy or hard, life requires that we take that step, and trust that the means to do so will be there when we need them.

This space I call WhisperZone. It's located on the Internet at www.WhisperZone.org where I share what is possible when we express the mastery at our core.

WhisperZone will provide a home for those want their inner voice to guide them through life. Not to some place determined by me or anyone else, but to the place their souls call for each to go.

Our motto at WhisperZone is, "Know your own way." After all, that's what life is about -- going where you were born to go.

It all starts with your next step. That step starts now as you wonder what to do now that you have read *Whispers in the Silence*. Will it be just another book that you set aside and forget? Or will you begin that inner journey to which it points?

If yours is to take the first halting steps into your own self-knowing, then you'll be glad to know you aren't the only one who's doing it, and that there is a place you can go for support and training targeted to your needs.

You'll also want to know a community is forming around this message, supporting each other and showing the world how to trust in the voice that speaks from the silence. For that is precisely what it needs to evolve into a higher expression of love than the conflict that marks man's history.

If you hear your inner voice, or want to, won't you join us? Help us build this vision of a world committed to its highest possibilities, where inner purpose integrates with the outer expression of life.

Why not come by and check us out? We have reserved a seat just for you.

At the very least, you'll want to receive my Whisper Report to help you keep on track. You can sign up for it at WhisperZone.

Until then, go with love -- for yourself and the world. For we are all one in the light.

I am

John

Index

A
abundance, 192
acceptance, 101, 103–106
addiction, 126
after-life, 48
Allah, 189
answers, 45, 50, 188
attachment, 13-14, 31, 33, 45-46, 131-132
attention, 92, 161
attitude, 128–129
awakening, 27, 59
  and alignment, 141
  and truth, 114
  by yourself, 71
  path of, 9-10, 40, 50, 170
  pre-awakening, 45
  process of, 41, 125
  seed of, 28, 79–80, 98
awareness, 27, 51, 92

B
balance, 168, 175

beliefs, 163–164
  orderly structure of, 46
biases, personal, 116
blame, 84-85, *see also* responsibility
Buddha, 187

C
celtic cross, 187
centeredness, 129
chance, 181
change, 56
character, 124
charity, 103
choice, 68
choices, 133
coincidence, 47, 181, 184
compassion, 187
concentration, 139
conflict,
  removal of, 170
  growth through, 169
consciousness, 39, 47, 66, 135, 167-168

higher, 89
   true nature, 70
contemplation, 81
contentment, 125–126
control, 52
covetousness, 123–124
cravings, 123–124
creation, 65–68
crisis of confidence
   in religious institutions, 20
criticism, 111
curiosity, 60
cynicism, 43, 155-156

D
Day of Judgment, 29
desire, 96, 168-170, 178
   and stealing, 117
   breaking holds of, 119-122, 182–183
   for personal gain, 170
detachment, 131-133, 170, *see also* letting go
discontent, 59-60, 125
Divine Plan, 29, 31, 59, 127, 160, 181, 190
Divine Will, 55, 133, 170, 190
doubt, 163

E
ego, 60
egocentric view of life, 13-14, 155-156, 167-168
emotions, 135–141
   anger, 140
   appreciation, 92
   arrogance, 110
   blame, 84–85
   compassion, 101–103
   control, 84
   control over, 182
   controlling, 136–141
   definition, 136
   desires, 52, 68, 86-87, 91
   disappointment, 45
   dissatisfaction, 41
   forgiveness, 101, 106–108
   gratification, 87
   guilt, 105
   impatience, 72
   love, 95–99
   overcoming, 135–141
   resolve, 72, 189
enlightenment, 59, 89–90, 178–179, 181, 189
entanglements, 169, 174

F
failure, 179
faith, 124, 164, 185-186, 191
fear, 27, 30
   of failure, 71
   of the unknown, 51, 70
forgiveness, 101
   and love, 106
free will, 83–87,
   see also choice, power of
future, 31, 90-92, 193
   and danger, 30

G
God, 11–12, 187

described, 23
gift of love, 97
grace of, 72–73, 87
image, 65
meaning and purpose, 16
Plan, 53, 67–68
see also Source
Golden Rule, 112
gratification, 41, 56, 87
greed, 14, 15
growth, 169, 184, 191
grudges, 106

H
habits, 79, 124
harmlessness, 109–110
harmony, 171
health
  emotional, 43
  physical, 43, 80
Holy Grail, 77
honesty, 116
hope, 53

I
inequities, 15
influence, circle of, 175
integrity, 114
intelligence, 66
intention, 159–162
  to find, 55
intuition, 52, 57, 73, 155-157, 175
  as testing tool, 80
isolation, 39

J
Jesus, 22–23
  and judgment, 106
  and love, 95
  in service to God, 53
John, 65–66
judgment
  as tool of aggression, 104
  of self, 105–106

K
karma, 32, 86–87, 190
karma-manas, 114
kindness, 124
knowledge, 30, 56, 128, 146

L
letting go, 190, *see also* detachment
life
  meaning of, 191
  purpose, 127
light, 187
  and religious institutions, 19
  message of, 9
  path of, 21, 84
  points of, 67
  seeking the source, 55, 153
living in the present, 89–93, 174
  and forgiveness, 107–108
  and meditation, 150
  and self-judgment, 105–106
love, 95–99, 154, 185-187
  and acceptance, 103–106

and compassion, 101–103
and forgiveness, 106
as tool, 171
lessons of, 170
the way of, 10–12

M
Maltese cross, 187
man, nature of, 40, 44, 61
man, purpose of being, 52
maya, 26, 143–144, 147
meditation, 140–141, 149–151, 187
mind
  freeing, 91
  influence of, 28
  inquiring, 49
  interpretive, 146
  rational, 46
  seeking, 46, 47
  untrained, 80
mindfulness, 137–138, 140
Mohammed, 187
Moses, 187
motivation, 16, 131

P
passion
  living with, 173–175
past, 90, 91–92
patience, 179
peace, 85, 125-126, 169
peace of mind, 45
perception, 26, 122, 143, 145
persistence, 177

personality
  evaluation of, 183
  integrated, 168
presence, 90
present, 30
purity, 125
purpose, 159, 160, 181

Q
questioning, 20

R
reincarnation, 32, 177–178, 190
relationships, 167–172, 174
religion, 185
religious institutions, 19–20
renewal
  source of, 81–82
resolve, 191
responsibility, 15–16, 21, 23, 78, 83-85, *see also* blame

S
sacrifice, 191
salvation, 17, 47
sarcasm, 110
seeking, 55-57
self-assessment, 40, 78
self-control, 125–126
self-deception, 78
self-examination, 78
self-fulfilling prophesies, 161
self-image, 95, 110–112
self-indulgence, 14, 182
self-judgment, 144

sensation, 145–146
separateness, 169
serenity, 70,
  see also peace
service, 30, 72, 127–128
silence within, 81
simplification, 173
sins, 98
social restraint, 170
social unrest, 15
soul, 61, 187
  belief in, 49
  calls to service, 170
  cultivation of, 10
  finding, 56
  in God's Plan, 67–68
  influence of, in life, 21
  journey of, 9
  needs of, 174
  purpose, 69
  urgings, 170
  voice of, 12, 81, 127, 155-156
Source, 10–11, 27, 39, 153
  see also God
spirit, 21, 61
  and peace, 22
  devaluing, 110
  dwelling place, 89
  existence of, 26–27
  in God's Plan, 67–68
  light of, 189
  love of, unconditional, 97
  way to, 30
  world of, 187
spiritual compass, 85

spiritual path, 175
spiritual relativism, 46
spiritual transformation, 16–17, 19
spiritual wilderness, 174
stealing, 117–118, 123–124
success, 71, 179
suffering
  inflicting on others, 13

T
technological advancements, 15–16, 29, 173
The Word, 65–66, 153
thought patterns
  and emotional upset, 139
transformation, 70–71
  and truth, 114
  by love, 97
  journey of, 78
  spiritual, 16-17, 19
trust, 191
truth, 46
  and white lies, 115
  process of finding, 114

U
unawareness, 25
uncertainty, 31
unification, 147–148
unity, 172
utopia, 27

V
violence
  cycle of, 13

W
wandering, 13, 79
will, 121–122, 133, 178
  asserting our, 104
  free, 83–87
  interaction of, 170
  spiritual, 66
  to live, 120
wisdom, search for, 56

Survey

Please take a moment to copy and complete the following survey.

Please give us a testimonial to help others who may come across *Whispers:*

_____
_____
_____
_____

May we use your name?   ☐ Yes   ☐ No

Name _____
City & State: _____

How may we contact you?

Telephone _____
E-mail _____

What did you like most?

_____
_____
_____

What did you like least?

_____
_____
_____

What questions were left unanswered?

_____
_____

What other books or products would you like to see?

_____
_____

Whispers' message of awakening is spread person-to-person around the world. Please tell your friends.

Fax to (954) 337-2300

Meet the Author

Mystic. Poet. Spiritual warrior. The labels are many, but behind them all is a master teacher of amazing insight and knowledge who shines a light so others can awaken to their own spiritual journeys.

A lawyer turned spiritual teacher with intensive training in the martial arts, meditation, and the movement of energy, John Dennison is a true Renaissance man who has pursued knowing for over half a century. Blessed at an early age with the perfect blend of intellect and intuition, he sacrificed his higher connection to a system of legal thought that left him alone in the darkness.

Rising to the challenge, John devoted himself to the affairs of mind and will, amassing extensive real world experience in the ways of law, business and finance. There he fought battles, negotiated million dollar deals, and helped people preserve the lives they worked so hard to build.

Never one to turn his back on his community, John freely served in leadership positions for organizations like the American Cancer Society, American Heart Association, Leukemia Foundation, Deaf Services Bureau, various schools, a federal credit union, business and investment associations.

After 25 years in the law, John had an epiphany that revealed a past life and purpose to serve carried forward into this life. Since then, he has devoted his knowledge and insights to share a new perspective on life and how it can heal the suffering that plagues mankind today.

Coming Soon!

Upcoming Books to Awaken Your Soul

If you liked *Whispers in the Silence*, you'll LOVE John's upcoming books from WhisperZone!

- **Journey of the Soul.** John lays out the evolutionary journey of the soul through which we know ourselves and add our piece to the Divine puzzle. *Journey of the Soul* details the process and sheds light on the lessons that face us all.

- **Windows of Awakening.** A compendium of John's best poetry on life and love, *Windows of Awakening* shows a side of John – and life – that few rarely see. Share the experience and let his heart touch yours.

- **Addicted to Suffering.** Mankind is addicted to suffering, and it shows in all aspects of our lives. That need for suffering puts us in a constant state of conflict within, as well as with the world around us. Here John shows how to recognize its symptoms and free yourself from its devastating impact on life.

Get them at your favorite bookstore.